# A Gift
# from Darkness

Also by Andrea C. Hoffmann

*Raif Badawi, The Voice of Freedom: My Husband, Our Story*
*The Girl Who Escaped ISIS: This Is My Story*

# A Gift from Darkness

## How I Escaped with My Daughter from Boko Haram

PATIENCE IBRAHIM

with Andrea C. Hoffmann

*Translated by Shaun Whiteside*

Other Press
New York

Library of Congress Cataloging-in-Publication Data

Names: Ibrahim, Patience, author. | Hoffmann, Andrea
   Claudia, author. | Whiteside, Shaun, translator.
Title: A gift from darkness : how i escaped with my daughter
   from Boko Haram / by Patience Ibrahim and Andrea C.
   Hoffmann ; English translation, Shaun Whiteside.
Other titles: Die Hölle von innen. English
Description: New York : Other Press, 2018. | Translated from the
   German. | "Originally published in German as Die Hölle
   von innen: In den Fängen von Boko Haram, by Deutscher
   Taschenbuch Verlag, Munich, in 2017." | "First published
   in English in Great Britain by Little, Brown in 2017."
Identifiers: LCCN 2017020688 (print) | LCCN 2017021969 (ebook)
   | ISBN 9781590518502 (ebook) | ISBN 9781590518496 (pbk.)
Subjects: LCSH: Boko Haram. | Kidnapping victims—Nigeria. |
   Terrorism—Nigeria. | Islamic fundamentalism—Nigeria. |
   Women—Nigeria—21st century. | Mothers—Nigeria—21st century.
   | Nigeria—History—21st century. | LCGFT: Autobiographies.
Classification: LCC HV6433.N62 (ebook) | LCC HV6433.
   N62 B653 2018 (print) | DDC 363.32509669—dc23
LC record available at https://lccn.loc.gov/2017020688

# Contents

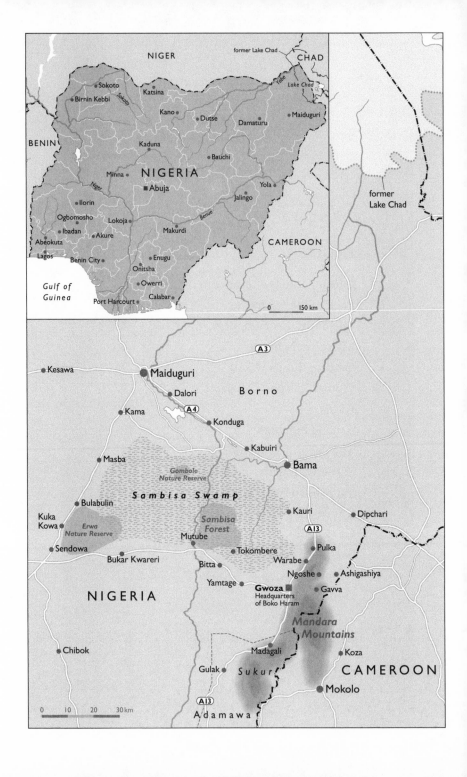

# Prologue

My husband's corpse lies on the beaten-earth floor of our shop. The air is full of the metallic smell of blood, which I know only from the few occasions when rich neighbors have slaughtered a cow.

They came on motorbikes, killed him and disappeared as quickly as they came. I watch the last of the blood seeping into the dirt, but I can hardly understand what's just happened: Islamist Boko Haram fighters have murdered my husband, just like that. Just because he was a Christian.

At that point I had no idea just how merciful his death was. At that time I would never have been able to imagine, when I lamented the loss of my husband in that modest board shack, that I would one day envy him his quick end. I didn't know my real martyrdom was yet to come.

# Journey into the unknown

I've only ever confided my plans to a few people. But now things are out in the open and I have to speak plainly, at least to my travel agent. "I want to go to Maiduguri," I say, as nonchalantly as possible.

"Where?"

"Maiduguri in Nigeria," I say, hoping faintly that the poor phone connection is the reason for her question.

"You're not serious, are you?"

Sabine, the owner of the little agency in Munich, is used to me by now. She's been booking my flights for years. And they have regularly taken me, as a journalist and an expert on Muslim terrorism and victim traumatization, to troubled regions of the world that no one would normally visit if they didn't have to. Sabine has organized my frequent trips to Afghanistan, Iraq or Africa without batting an eyelid. But she's unhappy about today's request.

"Maiduguri airport's been bombed," she informs me. "As far as I know nobody flies there anymore."

"Oh." I didn't know that. "Is there a northbound bus connection?"

"Are you crazy? It's about six hundred miles away from Abuja. And anyway . . ."

"Yes, you're right," I cut in. Sabine doesn't need to say any more. It would be too dangerous to drive through Nigeria by car. The A13, the main connection with the northern cities of the state of Borno, also lies on the road on which the terrorist group Boko Haram is active. It leads straight by the notorious Sambisa Forest. This swampland is where they have been holding the schoolgirls they abducted from Chibok, nearly seventy miles south of Maiduguri, in the spring of 2014, in an act that brought the terrorist militia into the world's eye. Michelle Obama, then the First Lady of the USA, put herself at the head of the "Bring Back Our Girls" movement, with which parents are trying to free their children from the clutches of the terrorists. Am I going to have to forget my travel plans?

"Let me just check," Sabine says. I hear her keyboard clicking. "Hm, you might be in luck: the Nigerian company Medview recently started flying into Maiduguri again, but quite irregularly. The flight might be canceled or postponed at short notice if the security situation gets worse."

"OK, great!" I hear myself saying. "Can you book them from here?"

"I can try." More clicking at the other end. "It seems to be working," Sabine says. "Do you want me to book it? Or just reserve it for now?"

"No," I say firmly. I've been dithering for long enough. For over a year I've been considering traveling to northern Nigeria. Since the Islamists of the Boko Haram sect in the north of the country began wreaking their havoc, and particularly since the kidnap of the Chibok schoolgirls, I've thought more and more about interviewing the female victims of the terrorist group. For a foreigner, and a white-skinned woman, such a journey is an incredibly risky undertaking. But recently I've found someone who knows the area to come with me: I can travel with Renate Ellmenreich, a retired Protestant vicar who lived there as a missionary years ago, and who still has good connections.

"I'm quite sure," I say to Sabine. "Book two tickets for me."

About a month before this I met Renate for the first time at Berlin's Central Station. Even though we'd only previously spoken on the phone, I recognized her straightaway. She was wearing a tweed jacket and a huge pair of purple sunglasses. The sixty-five-year-old strode energetically toward me, her freshly blow-dried pageboy cut bouncing in rhythm. "I'm Renate," she said in her sonorous vicar's voice.

When we're sitting in a café a few minutes later she tells me about her time in Nigeria. Around the turn of the millennium she and her husband were sent there by the mission in Basle. Renate was assigned to the station in Gavva, a small town at the foot of the Mandara Mountains, seventy kilometers southwest of Maiduguri. Her husband, Gunnar, took a similar job in Mubi, a little further to the south.

With a pencil, Renate does me a quick sketch of the area on a paper napkin. "Gavva's here," she explains, and draws a rectangle toward the top left-hand side of the district. "And this is the Sambisa Forest, about ten miles away as the crow flies." I'm startled by the small distance between the two places. Renate's chosen home in Africa is in the middle of the territory where the Islamic sect is terrorizing the population.

"We would never have expected anything like this," admits Renate, who was doing Christian development work. "Even then there were sporadic tensions between the Christians and the Muslims. But terrorism, and on this scale, was completely unimaginable."

At that moment a group of football fans drifts past us, shouting, waving the red and white flags that identify them as Bayern Munich supporters, and roaring their slogans. We have to interrupt our conversation. But Renate just smiles mildly. "Football is mostly harmless," she says. "But it's a different story if you give those young men a gun. In Nigeria, sadly, there are far too many men with guns. And it's always the women who pay in the end."

Renate lost her husband in Nigeria back then. He died in 2004 of a brief but violent fever, caused by a tropical virus. After that she set up an aid organization for widows. Now that organization looks after women victims of Boko Haram terrorism. "I urgently need to get back to Maiduguri to find out what the women there need most urgently," she tells me, deeply concerned.

"Then let's go together," I suggest. The fact that Renate has a local infrastructure of private contacts also brings the journey into the realms of the feasible as far as I'm concerned. "We can depend on your people there, can't we?"

"A hundred percent," she says, without hesitation. "But let's be clear about one thing: churches and vicars are high on the list of the terrorists' targets. And foreign journalists come next."

Even though I knew that, of course, Renate's words from our first conversation go on echoing in my head for a long time. But they won't put me off. Now we both have our tickets and our visas. She's given me precise instructions about what I need to pack: nuts, dried fruit, muesli bars, multivitamin tablets, protein shakes, bedsheets, towels, disinfectant spray, bandages, antibiotics, a mosquito net and—very important—instant coffee for our breakfast.

The food supply situation in the northeast of Nigeria is extremely poor. Since Boko Haram occupied large stretches of the terrain in 2014, the farmers haven't been able to work their fields, and harvests have failed. Food from the rich south comes to the north very rarely. First of all because there are road blocks and many attacks on transports. And also because there are hardly any solvent customers in the corrugated-iron metropolis of Maiduguri. The city is full of refugees who depend on government handouts.

In November 2015 we meet at Frankfurt airport. I've just come from Berlin, and as always I've allowed a very short transfer time. Breathlessly I dash into the departure lounge and look out for Renate. She hobbles toward me on crutches. She sprained her ankle the previous day. But clearly it didn't occur to her to cancel the trip. "The swelling's already going down," she reassures me, and cheerfully waves her crutches in the air. "I don't really need these things. But somebody in Nigeria is bound to have a use for them."

I grin. Now I'm quite sure that Renate's exactly the right traveling companion for me.

It takes our Lufthansa plane only six hours to get to Abuja, the seat of government and the second largest city in Nigeria. We get there at four o'clock in the afternoon local time. Hard to believe there is not even a time difference with Germany.

I step onto the escalator behind Renate and her crutches, and crash into a wall of tropical heat and high humidity. In the hall with the luggage carousels helpers run about busily to take our luggage outside on their trolleys in exchange for a few cents. They make an enormous racket. The only problem is: Renate's suitcase hasn't arrived. The big one, stuffed with the things that she needs for the job-finding workshops that she wants to do with the women in Maiduguri. Now we lack both the ingredients for soap production and the molds for muffin baking; these two skills were intended to enable the women to earn some money. Renate is in despair. "I can't travel on without my suitcase," she tells me.

We hastily fill out a series of very complicated forms to report the loss. A young woman in a pretty straight-hair wig is very helpful to us. "You might get your suitcase tomorrow, ma'am," she says, looking as if she doesn't believe it herself. "If you like, I can keep your claim slip and pursue the matter for you at the airport. Just write your phone number on it."

"My phone number?" Renate thinks for a moment. "Yes, OK." She writes down the phone number of her German friend Annegret, who lives on a farm near Abuja. We will spend the first night at her place. The sixty-year-old South German is waiting for us in the arrivals hall.

A little later we are sitting in Annegret's rickety Fiat. It's already getting dark. The road to the farm is quite heavily used. It leads through several small villages whose centers are recognizable by the gatherings of people and the proliferation of stalls. They are selling groceries, warm food and all kinds of paraphernalia. We buy a SIM card for Renate's phone. Then we turn on to a gravel track. From now on there are no villages; the bush used as pasture by the Fulani nomads stretches out on either side of the road.

Nigeria's population consists of a great variety of ethnic groups who speak a total of 514 different languages. The Fulani and Hausa in the north, who constitute about a third of the population, are among the biggest and most politically influential. They are Muslim. The south is dominated by the Christian Yoruba and Igbo, who each constitute about 20 percent of the overall population. About 180 million people in all live in Nigeria. Around half of them are Muslims, 45 percent Christian, the rest follow traditional African religions. In many places, however, widespread animist thinking mixes with the ideas of other religions.

We reach a grove of palm trees—and the road becomes even bumpier. Annegret skilfully drives around the potholes. When she stops somewhere in the darkness at last, I curiously open the door and step outside. A sweetish fragrance hits me with the warm evening air. It is very quiet. The only sound is the quiet rustle of the palms.

"Welcome to Hope Eden," she says.

Annegret leads us to one of the round huts that she and her husband, Shekar, rent to guests. It's made of red bricks that they bake themselves on the farm. Mosquito nets are stretched over the windows. There is no running water, but there's a big barrel from which water can be drawn, including the water for the toilet flush. Electricity comes from a solar cell on the roof.

At dinner in the main house lots of children join us at the table. They're all little relatives of Shekar that the couple have taken in so that they can go to school. Their own parents wouldn't be able to afford it. There is cassava with beans from the farm's fields. "And you just left the receipt with that woman? Even though you don't even know her?" she asks. "How is she even going to get in contact with you? We have no phone reception here on the farm."

"Oh my. And internet?" Just in case we don't get the suitcase in time I need to rebook our onward flights at midday tomorrow with an email to Sabine. That would definitely be easier than trying to find the relevant office somewhere around here.

Annegret smiles. "No, there's no internet. For that you'd need to go into Abuja. It's in the opposite direction from the airport. It's about an hour to the center."

Renate shakes her head. "Let's just try our chances at the airport."

The next morning we are woken at dawn by all kinds of noises that sound like a jungle: the grove of palm trees coos, buzzes and chirrups. Annegret, who is already feeding her schoolchildren, helps us to our feet with freshly brewed coffee. It tastes delicious. "Enjoy it," Renate advises me, "we won't be getting anything like that in Maiduguri."

We set off immediately after breakfast. There is no public transport, such as an airport bus. So to avoid being a burden on our host we hire a car and driver from the village. "If it all goes wrong, just come back to me," Annegret says as we wave goodbye.

On the way, Renate keeps trying to get through to the woman at the airport, on her mobile phone with the new SIM card, but to no avail. "Maybe she hasn't got up yet," I wonder after the fifth attempt, "or . . . "

"Or she's conned us," Renate says darkly. "We've been a bit naïve. With that form she could take legal possession of my suitcase whenever she liked. There's not a thing we can do. Why didn't we try her number yesterday?"

I can't give her an answer to that one. "Maybe we'll find her at the airport," I say, trying to reassure us both.

We get there a short time later. But there's nothing going on at that time of day. Since no planes leave in the morning, the counters at the international terminal are all bolted shut. And of course there's no one we can ask about the suitcase.

Renate and I are at a loss. She slumps exhausted on a bench and guards our luggage while I try to rebook our tickets in the national terminal. There are crowds of people at the Medview counter. I plunge into the crowd and fight my way to the front. It smells of sweat, perfume and deodorant.

"The tickets!" the man from the airline demands when I finally manage to attract his attention amid all the competitive customers. Luckily the official language in Nigeria is English, so at least we're able to communicate with one another.

"We have e-tickets." I hand him my phone, on which the tickets are stored. He frowns. He definitely wants to see a piece of paper. But I haven't got one. Then he passes my phone to one of his colleagues behind the counter. They chat together, looking rather skeptical. "Where did you book these?" the first one asks.

"In Germany."

"Paid for already?"

"Yes, of course."

"But the numbers don't agree with our system."

Oh, great, I think. What's that supposed to mean? Is he trying to tell me that the tickets I bought in Germany are invalid? "That's impossible," I protest helplessly. "Please look again!"

My phone wanders from hand to hand all around the airport, with me running after it. At least a dozen men stare at the document from abroad that's stored on it. It feels like hours until at last they find someone who's able to convert the international booking code into a local one—and who demands a healthy sum of money in return. I pay up.

But by now it's almost half past ten. Do we even have time to postpone the flight for another day? Just as I want to ask this awkward question, Renate hobbles up on her crutches. She is beaming. "The lady from the luggage office came," she cries, "and the suitcase is there too!"

"So I don't need to rebook?"

"No, it's all fine!"

She points to a young man who's come behind her to the counter with a trolley: all our luggage is stacked up on it. He zealously heaves our cases on to the scales, and wants to be rewarded accordingly. A hefty charge is also leveled on our excess baggage.

This is the first personal lesson that I learn about Nigeria, which enjoys the dubious reputation of being the most corrupt country in the world: there are lots of problems and there are lots of people who make money from solving those problems. Everything costs money. That's how the system works.

Then we're on the Medview plane. I haven't a clue why the company should be called "Mediterranean view." From the window I see the skyscrapers and the mosques of Abuja, whose domes gleam in the distance. And the vast outskirts of one-story houses that twist around the metropolis and spill further and further into the bush. The houses become increasingly humble the further they are from the center. The huts of the people who have moved from the country form the outermost ring around the city.

When we've left even those behind, the land is more sparsely populated. Near Abuja the soil is still fertile and many of the fields grow maize or cassava. But the further north we fly, the sparser the vegetation. Soon there are only very scattered trees in the steppe-like landscape, through which the Fulani nomads drive their herds of thin cattle. The lack of rain has dried the ground out—even though the dry season has only just started. Everything seems to have the same earth-colored tone.

At last it becomes hazy. It looks as if a veil has settled over the earth. At first I think it must be clouds. But strangely they don't part even when the plane begins its descent.

"That's bad luck, the harmattan has started already," Renate says.

"The what?"

"The desert storm."

I look out the window again. What to European eyes looks like mist or fog is really very fine particles of dust. They give even the strongest African sun barely a chance to reveal its power. "And how long does it last?"

"About a month. It's a phenomenon that occurs all over Africa. During the dry season the wind stirs up sand from the Sahara, which is then suspended like this over large parts of the continent. But it also helps to fertilize the fields with good loessic soil," she explains. So the harmattan will come with us on our journey.

The plane judders as we approach the ground. A herd of goats on the edge of the runway flees. The asphalt is warped or burst in many places. Still the pilot manages to bring the plane down safely. Renate and I look at each other.

"So, we're there," she beams.

We climb down the gangway, Renate still on crutches. We look around curiously. The airport building is right in front of us: a charred structure scattered with bullet holes, all its windows gaping. These are the traces that Boko Haram left in December 2013 when the group tried to overrun the town. I'm shocked by the destructive frenzy revealed by the serious damage to the building. You can't even get inside it. Instead we collect our luggage from a container that has been set up next to the demolished airport building.

While I trudge across the steaming airfield in the midday heat I become aware that Renate and I are actually the only foreign and white passengers who have strayed here: for that reason we are the only ones asked into a tent beside the container. Two Nigerian army officers want to see our passports. The officers ask us very seriously who we are, and what we plan to do here. Renate refers to her charity work in the EYN church, the "Church of the Brethren" that missionaries founded in 1923, and which now has around 350,000 members. The younger officer is clearly unimpressed. But the eyes of the older one begin to gleam. He assures us that we are most welcome.

Here in the north, where Muslims are in the majority, Christians form just fifteen percent of the population. Most of them only gave up their traditional beliefs a few generations ago. They are members of smaller tribes, who were chased by the more influential Kanuri. The Kanuri, whose kingdom was formed in the ninth century, ruled the Lake Chad basin and the north of present-day Nigeria for almost a thousand years. The pious emirs, who celebrated public prayer and Qur'an readings in their empire in the eleventh century, did a brisk trade across the Sahara. Their most important commodity was people who belonged to different ethnic groups and worshipped other gods. The Kanuri felt superior to them, and sold them as slaves to rich tribes and the Middle East. So it wasn't difficult for the Christian missionaries to persuade groups who had previously been hunted to adopt a different religion from their pursuers and oppressors when they came into contact with the modern world. In many places elements of traditional belief were preserved.

"He's probably a Christian himself," Renate whispers to me in German as our names are recorded by hand in a large book.

Then we step outside. Waiting behind a chicken-wire fence are Renate's friends and their companion: two women in tight, brightly patterned dresses and a young man in a white shirt and well-ironed flannel trousers. They have come to the airport with the police to collect us.

The younger of the two women, small and plump, in her thirties, waves to Renate from a distance and starts crying when she sees her limping. "Mamiiii! What happened to you?" Rebecca calls at the top of her voice.

"Not to worry, I can walk just as well without crutches," the vicar says, trying to reassure her. But Rebecca, Renate's closest colleague in Maiduguri, is inconsolable. And she gives free rein to her emotions. As we load the luggage onto the little bus, she sobs noisily. It's only when Renate throws her crutches in the luggage space and skips around the car park unaided a couple of times that she stops. "I only brought them along because I thought they might be useful to you," Renate says with a smile. Rebecca stares at her in disbelief for a moment, then laughs as well.

We sit in the back of the bus, another security measure. Because the windows are darkened, no one can see us from the road. As few people as possible are to get wind of our stay in Maiduguri. Curious, I look outside as we drive into the city through a big concrete gate. WELCOME TO MAIDUGURI, it says at the top of the arch. It's only at second glance that I see that it too is riddled with bullet holes. The frequent battles fought here between Boko Haram and the army have left their traces everywhere.

There's not much happening in the streets. Curious for a city whose inhabitants have trebled in number over the past few years to around three million because of the internal flow of refugees. There are hardly any street vendors, and there's very little traffic in the streets, but there are lots of military checkpoints: soldiers barricaded behind sandbags observe the traffic.

Occasionally they beckon a car out, demand to see the driver's papers and examine the chassis for explosives with their detectors. They're trying to filter out any possible suicide bombers. But in many cases they haven't managed to do that: here, on the wide boulevard built by the British, the Islamists bombed their way into the city only a few months ago.

Apart from these wide roads, however, there's little to remind you that the British, after their victory over the northern caliphates shortly after the end of the nineteenth century, extended their influence all the way here. Officially, in 1914 they united the protectorate of Northern Nigeria with the protectorate of Southern Nigeria into a single colony called Nigeria. Even so, until 1946 the north and south had separate de facto administrations. It was only in the last few years prior to independence in 1960 that the central administration became more heavily involved in the affairs of the north.

"But Boko Haram could never hold Maiduguri for long," says the young man sitting beside the driver and holding a walkie-talkie: Daniel feels responsible for our safety. He's an official of the Nigerian state and responsible for the refugees from the Christian villages.

We leave the boulevard and turn into a dusty side street. The road is uneven, and there is rubbish all over the place, plastic bags and bottles. The middle-class houses are behind high walls; they have carefully barricaded themselves in. A wall is going up around a school building, in front of which a group of little boys is playing soccer: parents and teachers want to protect their children from attacks. Boko Haram has particularly targeted churches and schools.

But then we pass by a school that hasn't succumbed to fear. Boys with white embroidered praying-caps and old-fashioned slates sit under a tree. The Qur'an students are writing suras on their slates and trying to learn them by heart. Beside them a teacher in a white robe with a stick in his hand keeps an eye on their progress. If they don't come up to scratch, it would seem that he probably sometimes resorts to the stick as well.

The boys are barefoot; their clothes are unwashed and threadbare. Many of them come from the countryside, from very poor conditions. Their families send them to the Qur'an school, but they aren't fed there and have to beg for their own meager subsistence. Some of them stand by the side of the road, pleadingly holding out their tin bowls. They ask for alms, something to eat. At first glance they look as harmless as all children. But it was here among the madrasas of Maiduguri that the Boko Haram movement formed and radicalized a few years ago, and it is here that it continues to enjoy its strongest support. Some of these boys in the threadbare shirts have, indoctrinated by their teachers or other radicals in the more extremist madrasas, already set off bombs in the market and killed all the bystanders. Their poverty makes them willing instruments of the Islamists.

The boys with the tin bowls look curiously after our bus as we continue on our way. At that moment I'm very glad that we're sitting behind darkened windows. We don't want word of our stay in the city to reach the Qur'an schools under any circumstances.

We pass by a residential estate for police officers and drive across an urban millet field piled high with rubbish. During the rainy season all of this land was under water. That was only a few weeks ago and may well explain why no one has built on the land.

Beyond the field begins the district known as Jerusalem, the Christian quarter. It's a poor, run-down part of town. We drive over a dusty field where several families are camped under the open sky, and head toward a big wall. We stop by the barrier. Daniel talks to the guards, who eye us with interest. A man with a detector looks under the vehicle for explosives—luckily he finds nothing. Then he lifts the barrier. We drive into a square enclosed by walls on all sides, at the middle of which stands a big whitewashed building with a tall spire at the side. This is the EYN church, the biggest church in Maiduguri.

We are staying at the home of the vicar and his family. The one-story building, with chickens and turkeys pecking in the sand in front of it, is right next to the church. Rebecca has arranged a room for us, one that the family doesn't use: she has had it painted and has brought a second mattress for me to sleep on while I leave the bed to Renate. In the adjoining bedroom a bucket with a ladle stands ready for washing. If we need hot water we're just to let them know in the kitchen.

"Do you think you'll be all right here?" Rebecca asks anxiously.

"Of course," we both reassure her. Inside the church compound we are guarded around the clock, which means that we're quite well protected against kidnapping, our hosts say. That's why they wanted us to stay here.

And for now we're glad we've arrived. We slump exhaustedly onto the mattress, and for the time being ignore the fact that we've crept into the eye of the hurricane.

We have an early start the next day. Shortly after sunrise there's a lot of activity outside the church. Goods are being unloaded, people are hurrying back and forth, and the women are busying themselves in the kitchen with big metal cauldrons. "It's harvest festival," Renate tells me as we sort ourselves out in our room. "Here it's celebrated after the end of the rainy season."

At that moment there is a knock at the door. Without waiting for an answer Rebecca storms in. She has smartened herself up and is wearing a bright orange dress. "Good morning, did you sleep well?" she says and sets a plastic thermos bowl down on the table. "Breakfast," she says, and opens the container, revealing a steaming white liquid with an aroma that is both sweetish and sour.

"Thank you!" Renate says, delighted. "This is *kunnu*, the breakfast here," she explains to me. "You really must try it."

"What is it?"

"A kind of porridge made of peanut butter, sugar and millet."

"Hm." I try not to pull a face when Rebecca holds the bowl under my nose and gives me a challenging look.

I hesitantly take a spoon. "It's good!" I lie.

"It gives you strength and keeps for ages."

"Hm." I'm secretly wondering how I can avoid having to eat it all. Renate guesses my thoughts.

"At least have a few spoonfuls," she commands. "Rebecca got up specially this morning to cook for us."

I nod. I bravely continue devouring the indigestible meal. My friend the old Africa hand seems to have no trouble eating this breakfast. "Hm," says Renate, but in a different tone to the one I just used. She actually enjoys this mush.

Then the celebrations begin. I'm wearing jeans and a T-shirt, just like yesterday, and I notice I'm getting disapproving looks. "Are you going to go to church like that?" Rebecca asks.

"Normally you would dress a bit smarter," Renate explains. She herself is wearing a colorful African dress that emphasizes her cleavage and her figure. "And you may have noticed that women here always wear dresses. Only prostitutes wear trousers."

"What?"

Rebecca starts laughing. "I'll have an African dress made for you," she suggests.

"Good idea," says Renate. She rummages around in one of her two enormous suitcases and takes out a beige and brown patterned top with a matching skirt. "And today you can wear this."

"Oh, that's lovely." I put the clothes on and the two women applaud.

"Properly African," says Rebecca. "Now you just need to have your hair done." She insists on plaiting my hair. Soon I'm wearing my hair in the kind of braids that would have been considered the height of modernity in Germany about eighty years ago. And we're ready to go, as far as she's concerned: we stroll across the yard in our party frocks to the church, from which the sound of rhythmical pop music is already emerging. The room is full to the rafters. People are even sitting outside the doors.

Some of the women recognize Renate from her time in Africa and wave to her. They clearly come from the villages that she looked after as a missionary. Now I understand why she chose this place as the base for her work with the Boko Haram widows: the EYN church in Maiduguri is the most important meeting point for Christian refugees from the whole region.

The service begins with the ringing of bells. When you bear in mind that the building is surrounded by mosques and Qur'an schools, the sound of the bells over the city is particularly loud and penetrating. The service lasts a whole four hours—and puts my patience sorely to the test. But the congregation shows no sign of tiring. People sing, pray and dance with an abandon that would hardly make you think many of them had recently lost family members, and had had to flee their villages to get away from the murderous gangs of Boko Haram. Even if many of them completely lost this year's vital harvest, worship still seems very important to these people.

Afterward the members of the congregation group together in the yard. Long queues form outside the kitchen. I recognize this morning's sweetish smell: the women of the congregation have made nourishing *kunnu*, a big bowl of which is handed out free to everyone as part of the day's celebrations. For many it will be the only meal they have today.

I notice a tall, very slender woman who is sitting all by herself on the vicarage steps and daintily eating her portion of *kunnu*. It's almost as if she has to force herself to eat. She wears a green floral dress and a headscarf in the same fabric. In a cloth tied closely to her back a baby sleeps. Rebecca calls to her in her language.

"That's Patience," she says, introducing the young mother. "She's a refugee and comes from the same region as I do: her village, Ngoshe, is only a few miles away from Gavva."

"Did they drive you out?" Renate asks.

"Worse than that. She was kidnapped," Rebecca answers for her. "Patience has seen terrible things."

The girl looks at the ground. "No good English," she murmurs apologetically.

"But now it's over. I've told her she must eat well," Rebecca says. She signals the women in the kitchen to give Patience an extra portion of *kunnu*. "That's important. Otherwise the breast won't produce enough milk to feed the child. Last week we had to take them both to the hospital because they were so weak."

"For heaven's sake," I say. "Does Patience have no relatives?"

Rebecca shakes her head. "No," she says. "She has no one now. No one but her little daughter."

The baby on the woman's back begins to giggle. She loosens the cloth and draws the little one tenderly to her. Two little hands reach hungrily for her breast—and for the first time I see the mother smiling.

At that moment I understand. Patience has survived for this little creature—an impression that her account of her experiences will confirm over the next few days. I ask her to tell me her story . . .

# Back to the beginning

No one in my village had expected to see me again so soon. In my parents" round hut they were anything but delighted when I was suddenly standing in the doorway.

"What are you doing here?" my father asked; he had assumed I was in Damaturu, where my husband's shop was. The town was more than five hours away from Ngoshe by bush taxi. After my wedding ten months ago I had moved there with my new husband. I still remember the day when we had a big celebration in the church of Ngoshe and I—dressed all in white—was entrusted to the hands of his family. After that I hadn't seen my parents again.

"Have you had a fight with Yousef?" my father said suspiciously. "Has he been unfaithful to you? All men do that! If you think you can come back to us, you're wrong. Your place is now in his house. I can't feed any more hungry mouths here, you know that ... "

"But, Father!" I said at last, finding the strength to interrupt him. "I have no home anymore. Yousef is dead."

"What's that you say?" My father looked at me in disbelief.

"He was murdered yesterday. My parents-in-law sent me back to you."

My father was speechless. He ran frantically past me into the yard between our huts. The idea of a daughter he had already married off coming back home drove him out of his mind. It was also unusual for my parents-in-law not even to invite me into their house during the mourning period. My mother understood very quickly, and began weeping quietly inside the hut. "My poor child," she murmured. "What will become of you now?"

I had no answer for that.

"Will you take me back?" I begged my father.

"You haven't even given him a child," he grumbled. "No wonder your in-laws didn't want to have you."

"A child wouldn't change the situation very much," my mother said. And she was right: no one would have been very interested in a girl. But my in-laws would have taken a boy away from me as soon as he didn't need me anymore. Because a male child assumes the task of overseeing the conversation between future generations and the family ancestors. And that is extremely important.

Maybe I need to explain that in greater detail: here in Africa time goes backward. By that I mean that we don't live in expectation of the future, we want to go to the ones who lived before us: to our ancestors. We are descended from them and we move toward them in the course of our lives.

We return to them when the earth takes us back. But someone who dies and enters the *Zamani*, generally understood as
the past, goes on existing in the now-time for as long as there
are relatives who remember him—male relatives, of course.
That's why it's so important for a man to leave a descendant.
Because without him communication with the ancestors
is severed, they fall into oblivion and eventually become
ghosts of the *Zamani*: they can no longer move back and forth
between the worlds. This was the fate that now seemed to
present itself to my parents-in-law and all their ancestors.
And for that very reason it was a disaster for my husband's
family that he had died without issue. They couldn't console
themselves with the Christian promise of heaven either.

"Be glad that she hasn't brought a baby," my mother said to
my father. "That would cost even more money."

"That would have been the last straw, her turning up
with a hungry brat," he said irritably. But I knew that for my
parents the question of a child was only a sideshow. What
worried them most of all was that in our culture widows have
a terrible reputation: they are generally suspected of yielding
to the attentions of men in return for financial rewards. I had
heard that often, even though the subject hadn't affected me.
People said bad things about them, even though I'm sure that
many of them had no choice but to seek a lover if they didn't
want to starve. Of course I wouldn't do that.

"Let's pray that she doesn't bring shame on us," my father
said to my mother as if I wasn't there.

She ignored him. "Come in for now and let me touch you,"
she said to me and pulled me to her on her straw mat. Her

hands ran over my face and felt my body. After the birth of my sister Ladi, seven years older than me, she had gone blind. So it was very important for her to touch people. Her hands substituted for her eyes.

"You're not pregnant?" she asked.

"No, Mother. Not that I know ... "

"What's that supposed to mean?"

"No, I'm not pregnant."

I was quite sure, since I'd only just had my period. I told my mother, and she was relieved. But I notice that my certainty made her sad. No, I wasn't pregnant. I didn't carry within me the seed of life. And I myself was almost amazed that it mattered so much to me. Because I hadn't loved my husband particularly. When he chose me as his future wife a year ago and asked my father for my hand, no one had asked me if I wanted to marry. The fact that the applicant had his own shop had been enough for my father.

Still, in the months during which we lived together, we had got accustomed to one another. Yes, more than that: I had taken pleasure in the knowledge that he was by my side. Because his presence gave me a feeling of security. By day I had worked with him in the shop. In the evening I had cooked for him and at night shared his bed. That was how our whole life should have continued. I was deeply shocked that he was suddenly no longer there. So, secretly, I wished that something of him had survived within me. Something that would outlast his death. A little creature that might ease my loneliness.

When I lay in my mother's arms, all of these thoughts ran through my head. Now that I had been widowed at the age of only seventeen, would I ever have children? Or had my life come to an end along with Yousef's death? Had I missed my chance to found a family of my own? In Ngoshe and Damaturu I had seen widows in the street begging for alms because they didn't know what to live on. Did that fate await me too? What would happen now that my future had been extinguished only the previous evening?

Mother stroked my head and rocked me as she had done when I was still a child. And for the first time since the terrible night I relaxed and began to cry.

"It's all right, my child," she said. "It's not the end of the world ... "

But I was sobbing so loudly that all our neighbors must have heard.

"Don't worry," she said consolingly. "You're young and beautiful. The Lord has blessed you with so many gifts. I'm sure a solution will be found for you."

The familiar scent of her body gradually calmed me down. She dried my tears with her scarf.

"I'll pray for everything to turn out fine."

"Amen," I replied.


I wasn't invited to Yousef's funeral. Among our people that's an affair for the men. His relatives didn't think my presence was required. As we had only been married for a short time they still called me his "bride," and felt no obligations toward me. Particularly where the distribution of Yousef's property and mine was concerned: the bed we had slept in together was not to belong to me under any circumstances. And neither was the table or the gas cooker on which I had cooked for him. His parents, sisters and cousins grabbed everything they could lay their hands on. But they rejected me as an annoying appendage.

As a sign of my grief I sat on the ground outside our house—but I didn't stay there alone for long: my parents and brothers and sisters, neighbors and friends kept me company in turn. That was how they mutely communicated their sympathy. Tradition required me to sit on the ground like that for seven days. From the early morning until deep into the night I squatted there, sometimes with company, sometimes on my own. I only took a break at night. When the time was over all my bones hurt, but I felt relieved. From now on we didn't talk about Yousef. He had joined his ancestors. My life with him belonged to the past.

At home with my parents, as I soon established, since I moved out everything had stayed exactly as I knew it. We lived in modest circumstances. My father grew millet, like everyone in the village. Every family had its own little plot of land. Just before the start of the rainy season we broke up the stony ground with picks and planted the millet seeds in the earth so that it would sprout with the first shower of rain. Because the period of time during which the sky moistened the earth with rain and made it fertile was very short—and seemed to be getting shorter and shorter with each passing year.

All the family members helped with the work. During the summer rainy season no child from our village went to school, because there was so much to do. The teachers too had to work their fields. If a child did turn up at school, it was told to go and give them a hand. And of course the parents said that in that case they'd rather take advantage of their children's labor as well. My father said the same thing. So, along with my seven brothers and sisters, off I went to the field every day to remove the weeds that grew just as quickly as the millet, which in the end could be sixteen feet high. And we also had to make a lot of noise to drive away the baboons that wanted to pilfer the millet. There were lots of very cheeky, hungry monkeys in the mountains. They were a regular plague. But no one hunted them because their behavior was too human. No one could bring themselves to.

In the last days before the rain subsided we couldn't take our eyes off the field. Even at night my father stayed there to guard the valuable harvest. If we were lucky the cobs were already ripe when we cut them from the stalks. Otherwise they ripened and dried on the roofs of the huts, where we left them for a few days in the sun.

Then came the threshing, men's work. My father and uncle joined forces with other men from their initiation group to do this strenuous work together. The men who had been through the traditional rites of adulthood as a group stayed together for the rest of their lives. They stood with their flails in a circle around the big pile of millet cobs, which they threshed in turn to the rhythm of their songs. They spent whole days like that, until all the grains had been threshed from the cobs and the millet had finally been taken to the granary. In our case that was a small, round mud hut with no windows, which stood on oil-soaked feet as protection against vermin. We shared it with my uncle's family.

That was our treasure trove. The supplies that we kept in there had to keep us going throughout the whole of the dry season to the next harvest. Quite honestly, that was impossible. Because the yield from our little field wasn't nearly enough to feed a family of ten. My four brothers in particular were always very hungry. So our supplies were regularly used up sooner than they should have been. Then my mother would prepare a thin broth of fibrous millet stalks and tell us to collect leaves from the trees to bulk it out. At least that way we wouldn't go to bed hungry.

My father earned a little extra by making fly swatters. He plucked palm leaves and cut them into narrow strips. For the best possible result the leaves had to be as fresh and flexible as possible when he was weaving them. Once a week he put his products on a hand-cart and went to the market to sell them for 100 naira (about 30 cents) each. If no one wanted his fly swats he came home in a very bad mood. Then he would guiltily ask my mother to beg for alms outside the churches in the surrounding villages so that we wouldn't starve. Because she was blind, people would always give her a few *kobos* (small coins). That way the two of them managed to pull us through.

My family's economic situation improved a little when my eldest sister, Hannatu, left us. I was still going to school and must have been about eight years old. But I clearly remember coming home one afternoon and seeing my father sitting on the tree trunk in front of his hut, negotiating with a strange man.

Our home consisted of a yard and several circular huts made of mud bricks. The whole thing was enclosed in a thorny fence. We call a mud-hut yard like that a *kral*. Often the English word "compound" is used to describe the residential unit of a family or an extended family.

For us, mud huts are like the rooms of a big house: my sisters and I slept in one hut, my brothers in another, my mother in yet another. My father had a hut to himself as well. Their roofs were covered with millet straw that we regularly had to replace so that water wouldn't drip in during the rainy season and turn the earth floor into a mud bath.

The kitchen was outside, under a spreading neem tree. We lit the cooking fire between three stones. Next to it stood a small table with our crockery: three pots, a few plates and cups. That was it. When it rained, we stretched tarpaulins over everything so that nothing got wet.

We didn't have a "bathroom" or "toilet" in the European sense. But my father had dug a ditch behind the huts. It was covered with wood. In the middle of the cover was a hole for us to do our business, which we then covered with a lid. Beside that convenience was a bucket of water, as well as a piece of soap and a stone for rubbing off the calluses from the feet—everything you needed for a thorough cleansing.

We girls in turn fetched the water for washing and cooking from the well in the early morning. In the hot and dry season, however, it sometimes ran out, and then we had to walk all the way to the spring in the mountain. It spilled from the ground high in the hills, in a little low cave that you could only enter by bending your back. The path up there was steep and led past lots of rocks that you could only negotiate by skipping carefully from stone to stone with the twenty-liter bucket on your head. Of course that was very tiring, and took up almost half a morning.

As custom decreed, I brought my father and his guest some water to drink. As I did so, I heard them haggling. "I'll give you a cow for her," the stranger said.

"A cow and a goat," my father said.

"That's too much."

"Just a mark of acknowledgment for the fact that I've kept her fed for you for over ten years."

They reached a deal. On the evening of the same day my father told Hannatu that she was going to get married: he had found a good husband for her. Hannatu had no objections, as all her friends were getting married. Father spent the next few days building a little stable. Even before we celebrated the wedding, the man brought a cow and a goat, both of which had just given birth, and therefore gave milk. My father delightedly took delivery of the animals. Although he had to sell the cow soon afterward to tide us over, he was now one of the cattle-owners of the village—and our food situation began to improve slowly but surely.

About a year later Father married off my second-oldest sister, Ladi. And the same sequence of events repeated itself: for Ladi he got a cow and a goat once again, the standard price for a young girl. Two years later, when the time came to marry my third sister, Tani, five years my elder, the little stable was barely big enough, even though my father had occasionally sold animals in the meantime. I was very sad about Tani's marriage, because she was the nearest one in age to me and had almost brought me up. I loved her delicate, peaceful nature. When she left us, my father converted the hut where we had slept into a stable. I moved in with my mother. But as soon as I had reached the appropriate age, Father swapped me for a cow, a calf and a pregnant goat. That was a very good price.

The animals were still in the stable when I came home from my brief excursion into marriage. I had been catapulted back, as if by time machine, into a life that I had thought was a thing of the past. The situation was a bit too much for all of us, particularly my father. He didn't really seem to know what to make of the fact that I was suddenly back. He thought about what to do with me for a few days, and consulted his brother, who lived very close by. Then he made his decision.

One evening, when the sun set behind the mountains and our huts cast long shadows in the remaining light, my father and uncle called me in. They sat on the tree trunk in front of Father's hut and said they wanted to talk to me about my future. I became quite frightened when I saw their serious expressions. I nervously joined them.

"You know our family isn't rich," my father began.

I nodded.

"You are now an adult. It is very unusual for a married daughter to come home again ... "

"Yes, I know."

"But since it is so, you should make yourself useful and earn your own living. I can't afford to have you just living at my house and eating. After all, I spent a lot of money on your wedding. Money some of which I still owe your uncle."

I didn't know exactly what Father meant by that. As I had only gone to primary school for five years and hadn't learned a trade after that, he could hardly demand that I go after a job outside the house. And within our household I had always made myself useful: I had cooked, cleaned, looked after my mother ... What else could he demand of me?

"From now on I would like you to go working in your uncle's house," he said. "He will pay for your keep and feed you."

And the matter was decided. I wasn't asked if I agreed. My mother told me not to complain, because it could have been much worse. "Your uncle is a good man. You should be grateful to him. As a widow you should be glad that someone has taken pity on you. You shouldn't make too many demands on life."

I didn't. Without complaining I became housemaid to my uncle and his wife, but went on living with my parents. I don't know exactly why, but my uncle was financially a little better off than we were. He too was a farmer, but he had leased a more fertile field than my father. He also bred chickens, whose eggs he sold at the market. He owned an old moped that he was quite proud of. But at the moment he couldn't ride it. As the terrorists of Boko Haram traveled on motorbikes, our state government had imposed a complete ban on the use of them. He still had his mobile phone, with which he organized the sale of the eggs, among other things. As there was no electricity in his huts, he regularly had it charged in a shop. His three sons used the phone a lot as well. Two of them were still bachelors; the third lived with his wife and her baby in a hut of their own in the same compound. His daughters had already married and gone to other villages. That was why there was now a shortage of female labor.

I was the maid of all work, as I had been at my parents' house: I got up in darkness at four o'clock in the morning, dressed and walked to the village well to fetch water with a big bucket on my head. The well was about a half mile away from the huts. I met lots of girls my own age there. We chatted and exchanged the latest news as we filled our buckets. Of course the others had already heard about the blow that fate had dealt me. Many of them were also engaged or had just got married. The idea of losing their husbands as quickly as I had done was really horrific to them.

"And you were there when they killed him?" asked Rifkatu, a former classmate who had been one of the bridesmaids at my wedding. I could still see her in the beautiful dress that she had worn to the party, and felt suddenly sad. All the hope and confidence of that time had gone up in smoke.

"Yes," I said. "They did it in front of my eyes."

Rifkatu shivered involuntarily. "They are a terrible sect," she said, "they are completely mad. But people in Ngoshe wouldn't do anything like that."

"I hope you're right," I said doubtfully. Because by now I knew that Boko Haram worked on the quiet. Even the people that Yousef and I had dealt with in Damaturu had always assured us that the group had no support in the town. And then it had happened anyway.

"No, I can't imagine that," Rifkatu said, convinced. "We get on well here. I have lots of Muslim friends."

All the way home I brooded about whether she was right and we could really feel safe in Ngoshe—and reached no conclusions. The Muslims were in the majority in Ngoshe, we Christians in the minority. But in the past we had had hardly any problems with each other. There had been very little friction. And if there were any disagreements, they usually had less to do with religion than with concrete material issues. How can I put it? In local politics, the Muslims enjoyed some privileges over us Christians. Often their families were richer because they were closer to the emirs who used to rule in the north of Nigeria. Even today people join Islam if they want higher office or a career in politics. It's the only way. It's an unwritten rule that Muslims never allow anyone except their own into these positions.

Christianity, on the other hand, was adopted chiefly by the tribes who were in conflict with the emirs or oppressed by them. My own tribe, for example, the Ngoshe tribe, lived completely withdrawn in the mountains until the 1960s. Even today, logically enough, they don't have much power or wealth. Still some members of the tribe manage to work their way up and outrank the Muslims in material terms. That was what my husband Yousef had done, for example. And that was how he had earned their hatred. I was convinced that the Muslims of Boko Haram had murdered him not for religious reasons but out of pure envy.

Unfortunately there had also been similar events in Ngoshe. Did Rifkatu not know anything about that, or did she prefer to keep it out of her mind? No, I thought, she was deceiving herself: even though we had gone to school with the Muslims of Ngoshe, even if they were our friends, we couldn't feel safe here. When I walked past the dark mosque in the middle of the village, I noticed that my footsteps quickened involuntarily. Envy can poison the hearts of men. It already had.

Back in my uncle's *kral* I set down my water jug and put some wood in the stove. I didn't have to poke it for long before the logs caught fire. I had to hurry to make breakfast. First I ground the rough millet seeds with a pestle and mortar, then boiled them up with water. They had to simmer for about an hour. While that was happening I fed the animals. Right at the end I added some sugar, tamarind and peanut butter to the mixture in the pot, giving it a sweet and sour taste. My *kunnu* was ready in time for sunrise. My uncle and his sons, who by now had got up, crept hungrily around the fire. Before they set off to work in the fields they consumed substantial portions of food. *Kunnu* keeps you full for the whole day, which is why we love it. Because where there's *kunnu* in the morning, people are never hungry.

After the men had gone, my aunt and her daughter-in-law, Savan, came to have their breakfast. It was particularly important for Savan, who was my age, to eat well, as she was nursing an infant. I secretly watched her giving the child the breast after her meal. How lucky she was! But apparently she wasn't aware of it. She took her circumstances for granted. Probably I would have done the same in her position. Perhaps it's always like that: if happiness is there, you don't see it. In my marriage with Yousef I hadn't felt especially happy. I had seen it as my natural right to be married to a man and have children with him. It's only when happiness suddenly disappears that you understand what you had in your hands.

When everyone had finished eating, I scraped the leftovers out of the pot. I ate some of it myself, and put the rest in a little plastic bowl to bring to my mother later on. She often went without at home, as she always let the rest of us go first. Then I washed our pots and pans.

I usually spent the morning clearing up. Every day I took a broom and swept the whole of the yard, which was left in a poor state by rain or desert dust according to the season. I swept up all the leaves and twigs that had fallen from the neem trees during the night, and piled up the wood and leaves near the stove so that I could fire it up later on. (Neem trees are tall with dark green leaves and are hardy enough to grow in very dry areas. Their leaves are burned to chase away mosquitos, and they are also used in several local medicines.) Then I let the chickens into the yard and tied the geese to a tree outside so that I could clean out their houses.

By midday I was usually quite tired. When the sun had reached its highest point I would often sit down on a mat in the shade of one of the huts and lean my back against the mud wall to rest a little. Sometimes I even dozed off for a while. But my duties in the household were by no means over.

There was always something to do. Sometimes in the afternoon I cleaned the huts, sometimes I washed the clothes. That was quite tiring, as I only had very simple cleaning materials: I had to scrub each item of clothing individually with a lot of soap on the washboard to free it from dust. The next day my muscles always ached. Then I hung the washing out to dry on the fence between the huts.

In the afternoon, when the shadows grew longer, I walked to the well again, because by then I had used up all the water. Then I started preparing the evening meal. In the evening there was usually millet or maize. We ate rice or even a piece of chicken only on Sunday afternoon after the service.

Sunday was the highlight of the week. On Sunday I only did the minimum of tasks. Of course I had to fetch the water; I also made breakfast. But then I washed and put on my yellow floral dress, which I never wore on other days, to spare it for this occasion. When the bells rang, we all went to church together: my uncle and family, and my parents and my younger brothers, who still lived at home, all in their Sunday best. I loved it when we all turned up together as a clan like that. Because it meant I didn't feel alone anymore, but part of a community.

What I liked best about the service was the music. We had a pretty hot band and a church choir which would, every week, perform new pieces composed by its own members. I greedily absorbed their melodies and rhythms. Later, at work, I often found myself singing them to myself involuntarily, because they kept me company in my head for the whole of the next week.

That was how I spent my days. After only a short time it felt as if I had never left Ngoshe and my family. My brief marriage felt like a dream. I almost doubted that I had ever been married. But unfortunately that feeling was deceptive.

There was in fact one crucial difference from before: I was no longer one of the girls who hoped that one day a man would come and ask for her hand. My future prospects were worse than modest.

# The omnipresent danger

Patience and I meet in the church compound every day. She comes with her baby on her back and we sit down on the bench beneath the big neem tree. While Patience tells her story the child either sleeps or wriggles in her lap, looking at the world with big eyes. Seventy-year-old Asabe, a retired English teacher and the spokeswoman for the widows of Maiduguri, patiently translates each of her words for me from the Hausa language.

At first Patience finds it strange that I should be interested in her story. "What happened to me is nothing special," she says over and over again. "So many women were kidnapped or lost their families. Isn't it going to be boring if I tell you all that in great detail?"

"No," I assure her, "none of it is boring. People in Europe and the rest of the world don't know exactly what's happening here."

"Really?" She shakes her head in disbelief.

Patience finds it hard to think that she might be significant in any way: she's always been told that she's unimportant. So at first she can't really believe that I consider her story to be worth telling. She can't grasp the idea of the book that I'd like to write about it. The only book she knows is the Bible.

But still I notice that she likes me being interested in her. So she willingly joins in with the experiment. The very fact that someone is listening to her seems to be a completely new experience for her. And after a few days I notice that the young woman is starting to trust me. She no longer seems as shy as she did at first, and even looks me in the eye from time to time. Her story becomes more fluent. Sometimes she even laughs when I ask her a particularly stupid follow-up question. "What? You don't know how to plant millet?"

"No, where I live we hardly have any millet," I assure her. "Tell me about it, Patience! Describe to me exactly how your life here works."

"How it used to work," she corrects me. "Everything's changed in the meantime. Today we can't plant millet anymore. The fields are all left fallow and we have little to eat. It would be much too dangerous to go back to the villages."

Patience's remark brings me back to the present, an oppressive present. Because while we are spending our time together, the life—or perhaps I should say: murder—going on around us hasn't stopped. It goes on, undiminished, day after day. The Boko Haram terror machine is in full swing.

A wanted list with portraits of ninety-nine Boko Haram fighters hangs on the inside of the protecting wall that surrounds the church compound. The men on the poster are posing with machine guns. They are all armed to the teeth. Some of them give warlike grins to the camera, other photographs are blurred and clearly taken with a phone, or in passing. In the middle of the poster is a rather larger photograph showing Boko Haram chief Abubakar Shekau with his pointed cap: that notorious figure who presents himself to the public in his propaganda videos as a mixture of black magician and psychopath.

Everyone in northern Nigeria knows his brutal messages; they terrify people. "We long for battle, for attack and killing as we might long for delicious food. We believe in that and we fight for that," he announced in one of his videos in November 2014, a good six months after the spectacular abduction of the Chibok girls. "It is our goal that everyone on the whole planet will live according to the laws of the Qur'an." No wonder that Patience looks away in horror every time her eye chances to fall on the portraits of that man.

"Do you know them?" I ask Patience.

She nods. "Yes, I've seen them, some of them."

"Even that one?" I point at their leader, Shekau.

"In Ashigashiya. Yes, I think that was him: a terrible man."

It was also Shekau, the man with the pointed cap, who transformed Boko Haram into the killing machine that it is today: an army of an estimated 50,000 men who have sworn loyalty to Islamic State (ISIS). Well over two million people are on the run from these monsters.

The group was founded in around 2003 by the Wahhabi preacher Muhammad Yusuf, who demanded a pure, unadulterated Islam: in Maiduguri he raged first of all against the "superstition" of many Muslims in northern Nigeria, who had remained true not only to Muhammad but also to their ancient gods and traditions—and for whom a rain dance and a visit to the mosque were therefore not a contradiction. Not many of his coreligionists were very interested in that. But when Yusuf began to criticize the establishment and the Christian-dominated central government, it appealed to people, particularly young unemployed males.

The Muslim north is structurally the weakest region of Nigeria, and the people there feel chronically neglected by the politicians in the seat of government in Abuja. Here in the north the Muslim emirs held sway until the start of the twentieth century, and Western education was consequently prohibited. For that reason there is still a high educational deficit in the north even today: seventy percent of people can neither read nor write. Nigeria is the biggest economy in Africa, with a quickly growing GDP, but the wealth is distributed very unequally from region to region. In comparison with the rest of the country the Muslim north is dirt poor. The state is perceived as an exploiter. Nothing reaches the people here of the wealth from oil in the south. So Yusuf's question as to why some should live in expensive, guarded residences while others fetch their water from the well, fell on fruitful ground. Accordingly, he declared war on the "thieves" from Abuja.

When a demonstration by Boko Haram in Bauchi was banned in 2009 there was unrest, which spread to the whole of the north of the country. The army defeated the uprising and the sect leader, Yusuf, was killed. After that nothing was heard from his movement for a while. It was only a year later that Boko Haram was revived, this time under Shekau: his people began shooting local politicians from their motorcycles, setting fire to police stations and setting off bombs in the street. As these terrorist acts were also at first limited to the north of the country, the politicians in Abuja did nothing about them. But in the summer of 2011 Boko Haram moved on to suicide bombings and also attacked the capital. First they hit police headquarters, then the UN building.

Shekau declared a "religious war." "We have attacked no one but the Christians," he announced, explaining the violence. "Everyone knows what terrible things they have done to us. Everyone knows that the constitution is the work of unbelievers; everyone knows that the Western education system teaches things forbidden in the Qur'an. The only thing that we demand is that the will of Allah be respected. The work that we are doing is the command of Allah. Everything we do is written in Allah's book."

Shekau set out his goals very clearly. First, the introduction of sharia throughout Nigeria as an alternative to democracy, which supposedly privileged Christians in the south. Second, "May God bring death to us all if his laws are not respected"—with these words the sect leader was calling upon the Muslim population to make martyrs of themselves.

This was a declaration of war on central government—and a wake-up call for the politicians in Abuja. They could no longer ignore the problem. The fact that the terrorist organization still went on growing and gaining in strength for some time to come may have had to do with the involvement of many politicians with the secret association. "The challenge we have today is more complicated," the then president Goodluck Jonathan said in his New Year address in 2012, in which he referred to the Mafia-like structures of the country, saying that no one knew exactly who was involved: "Some of them are in the executive arm of government, some of them are in the parliamentary-legislative arm of government, while some of them are even in the judiciary. Some are also in the armed forces, the police and other security agencies. Some continue to dip their hands and eat with you and you won't even know the person who will point a gun at you or plant a bomb behind your house. That is how complex the situation is." At this point Shekau had already given the Christians in the north an ultimatum to leave the territory.

A year later Boko Haram changed tactics again and began to conquer whole tracts of the country in the north. Rumors circulated about a meeting in Mecca between Boko Haram people and representatives of ISIS, al-Shabab and al-Qaeda in the Islamic Maghreb. The Islamists were supposed to have discussed this tactic there, and voted on it. The territorial conquests of ISIS in Iraq, and of Boko Haram in Nigeria in the summer of 2014 underpinned the rumor of this agreement. Shekau declared his caliphate about two months after ISIS leader Abu Bakr al-Baghdadi did the same.

Within a very short time the man with the pointed cap managed to conquer a huge amount of territory in Nigeria. By the end of 2014 his empire was already the size of Belgium. Even experts were baffled as to how he could achieve this—and whether Shekau was receiving financial support from abroad.

The leadership structures of his organization are mysterious; no one knows precisely what they are. Supposedly several groups are acting independently of one another, which always represents a big problem in attempts to negotiate with Boko Haram: no one but Shekau, who in his videos repeatedly and categorically rules out negotiations, seems to have the authority to speak for the organization as a whole.

But it is not clear whether he did not become an imaginary figure long ago. The Nigerian secret services at any rate insist that the man who appeared as Shekau between 2011 and 2013 died some time ago: he is believed to have died on July 25, 2013, in the Cameroonian town of Amitchide, from bullet wounds inflicted on him by the army some weeks previously. Less than a month later he mocked the claims of his death in a short video: "We have killed countless soldiers and we will kill still more," he laughs. "Our military power is greater than that of the Nigerian army."

However, Nigerian secret service experts point out that the man who now appears as Shekau has a rather wider face than the original. His upper lip is thinner and his nose rather bigger. The army also claims to have killed this new Shekau in September 2014 in Konduga. But his ghostly video messages did not stop even after that.

The face of Boko Haram tirelessly calls for continuation of the bloodshed. "I enjoy killing the people that Allah commands me to kill—just as I like to kill chickens or sheep," Shekau I announced as early as January 2012. And Shekau III confirmed this view in November 2014: "Shekau eats the hearts of unbelievers, because unbelievers violate the laws of Allah."

This slaughter continues beyond the walls of the church compound while Patience and I talk and she tells me her story. And news of it penetrates our apparent oasis of peace, a deceptive peace. As we are cut off from any kind of internet communication, I learn of the terrible events from a newspaper that someone has left on the bench under our tree.

19 DEAD, 130 INJURED IN SUICIDE ATTACKS is the headline that leaps out at me on the morning of December 6, 2015. Horrified, I go on reading: the tragedy occurred the previous day in a small town on Koulfoua, an island in Lake Chad. It is just 125 miles north of Maiduguri. After Boko Haram had gathered more and more fighters in the area, a state of emergency was declared there a month ago. Civilians had sought refuge from the terrorists there. But that was where they sent their angels of death: four bombs exploded simultaneously amid crowds of people at a busy market. And then I read a detail that makes me shudder: the attack was carried out by women.

Patience isn't surprised. "The wives of the Boko Haram fighters are very violent," she says. "Many are converted while in captivity."

I look at her for a long time. "Did they try to do that to you too?" I dare to ask at last.

Patience looks at the dusty ground. "Yes, of course," she says quietly, rocking her child.

"Is it true that the Chibok girls were deployed in attacks like this?" I ask, as I have heard such rumors from many quarters.

Patience thinks it's very likely. "But not just them!" she says. "They have a huge influence on all the women and girls in their power. If a woman marries a Boko Haram fighter, she can expect that her husband will demand that she blow herself up."

Only six days later, on December 11, 2015, the Islamists strike once more in Nigeria. This time I find out from the vicar's wife. She looks very shocked and nervous after she receives a call from a relative on her mobile phone.

"What's up?" I ask her.

"They've attacked Kamuya," the vicar's wife tells me. The small village is only about thirty miles from Maiduguri. She has family there. "A dozen men arrived on bicycles and torched the whole village."

In the course of the day more and more details about the attack come to light. It was probably an act of revenge against General Tukur Yusuf Buratai: the most senior army officer in the state of Borno comes from the village of Buratai, only six miles away, which was also attacked recently. He had a second home in Kamuya—and now the villagers have paid for it. Fourteen of them didn't manage to get away in time. They were murdered in cold blood: seven of them were shot by the Islamists, the other seven were beheaded. Probably to give the fleeing inhabitants the most shocking possible sight on their return, the hacked-off heads were draped on the bloody torsos.

"It's terrible," the vicar's wife says, so quietly that I can barely hear her. "I just hope that they leave us in peace here in Maiduguri."

That is what everyone here is worried about. After the most recent attacks the atmosphere in the church compound is even more tense. The guards by the gate have stepped up their checks: no one can come in carrying a piece of luggage. But will this rule protect us if a suicide bomber really takes the EYN church as his target, I wonder? In the past Boko Haram has carried out numerous attacks on the churches of the Swiss missionaries in the area. Recently some girls who had previously been kidnapped carried bombs in their baby-cloths. Patience could easily have been one of those attackers.

Now, just before Christmas, it is particularly dangerous. In previous years particularly large numbers of churches have been attacked, set on fire or bombed. While in Europe and the rest of the Christian world decorations are going up in the streets, the northern Nigerian Christmas tradition seems to be to attack Christian places of worship. Everyone assumes that something's going to happen in the next few days or weeks. And I too am starting to feel really ill at ease. The attacks are coming closer. Did Renate and I do something incredibly reckless when we decided to come here at Advent, of all times? Were we able to judge the situation correctly from Germany?

"There's no point brooding about it," Renate says when we sit together in our room that evening and I hesitantly tell her of my concerns. Somewhere in the distance I can hear gunfire.

"What was that?" I ask her.

"No idea. Some sort of argument. I'm sure it's nothing. People here are quick to reach for their guns." I don't find that very reassuring. I listen hard and hope that Renate is right to be so confident. Eventually the shots fall silent. It's very dark now; in all likelihood they can't see their targets anymore.

From six o'clock in the evening there's a curfew across the whole town. That's when public life comes to an end: shops and stalls close with almost Swiss precision. That alone reveals the state of emergency in which the area finds itself, because as a rule not much store is set by punctuality. People hurry home. Anyone who fails to get there has to spend the night wherever they happen to be, if they don't want to get picked up by the army. There's no electricity from six o'clock either. At least not for people who don't have solar cells on the roof or their own generator. The state electricity company can only manage to supply power for a few hours a day.

On those long evenings without light and electricity Renate and I have no option but to retreat to our guest room in the vicarage. Since there is nowhere around where we could pick something up during the day, we eat the provisions that we've brought with us from Germany: mostly nuts and dried fruits. Thanks to Renate's long list we've packed plenty of those. If we're lucky, the vicar's wife or Rebecca will also give us a little rice or fried plantains. It's almost impossible to get hold of fruit or fresh vegetables; and in any case they're taboo because of the germs. Some days we manage to get hold of a tin of tuna or a loaf of white bread to pep up our meal.

*"Bon appetit,"* says Renate and raises her Coke can, her latest haul. Coca-Cola is available from the street stalls, as it is everywhere in the world.

Renate's shopping trips along the nearby streets and in the market are legendary in the church compound. Today, she says, she had a row with Daniel about it: the young civil servant whose duty it is to keep an eye on us doesn't want us to show our faces in the street, not even to buy a can of Coke or any other trifles. Renate, who is used to strolling about freely, thinks he's being unnecessarily cautious.

"The people are so friendly," she tells me. "They're glad that someone's come from outside at last and taken an interest in them."

"Yes, I know," I say with a grin. I've also accompanied Renate on her forays: she blossoms when she meets people and is able to talk to them. She says hello to everyone, pauses for a moment, has a little chat with the people in Hausa. The vicar listens to their problems and has a few words of sympathy for each of them. That must be how she approached people when she was a missionary.

But times have changed. "Boko Haram is everywhere," I remind her. Particularly here, in Maiduguri, the terrorist militia has eaten into society like a tumor, and invaded every family, every sphere of everyone's lives. Many people you wouldn't have expected it of are in secret communication with the Islamists and pass information on to them. There's no way of knowing who you can trust and who you can't. "We should stick to his instructions," I say, defending Daniel's position.

"It's not a great idea if word gets around Maiduguri that two white women are staying at the church."

"But I need ingredients for my next workshop!" she complains. She wants to make muffins with the widows, and is trying to find a local substitute for the ingredients in the recipe. It's hard to explain to Rebecca, who doesn't know what baking powder and vanilla extract are. Renate herself has to see what's on offer and then use her imagination.

But at least she seems thoughtful now. At last she agrees to be driven to the market next time rather than going on foot. At least that way she won't be seen going in and out of the church compound.

"That's a better idea," I tell her. "It means our hosts won't be put in danger either."

"Maybe," she complains. "But you can't control everything. The risk is just there, for a foreigner as well as for the people who live here."

She's right. There's no safety in northern Nigeria, nowhere. Certainly not in a busy market where hundreds of people are doing their shopping. It isn't even a month since a bomb last went off here.

Perhaps, I think to myself, you need to be a vicar to accept all that and carry on anyway.

# My second chance

After I got back the months went quickly. First we celebrated harvest thanksgiving, then Christmas. I got used to my new old life and tried not to rail against my fate. My family accepted the situation too. I assume that my uncle, who liked to present himself to my father as a benefactor, was secretly quite glad that he still had me working for him.

One afternoon I was, as so often, busy sweeping his yard, for the second time that day. In the middle of the dry season it was roasting hot and the area between the huts was full of fine sand that blew over to us from the desert. In principle I should have kept constantly starting my work over and over again because so many little grains were drifting through the air.

When I was sweeping up the dust into the dustpan, I heard men's voices nearby. I interrupted my work and listened to hear whether it was my uncle come back with his sons, or my father with his brothers. But these were strangers' voices. And since my bad experience in Damaturu I was a little nervous: even though we had no problems with our Muslim neighbors in Ngoshe, as I have said, I felt uneasy when strangers approached the property.

"Hey, girl!" I heard a man shout.

I turned round and saw him standing with two other men outside the gate to our yard: he was very tall, and his expression was open and direct. His skin was strikingly pale, which is considered attractive around here. A really good-looking guy, although not very young. I guessed he was about forty. "We are from the Zalidiva tribe in Gwoza," he said, introducing himself and his companions.

I didn't react.

"Hey, don't be so shy," he laughed. "Could the three of us maybe have some water? It's incredibly hot today."

I couldn't say no. In our tradition, travelers always have the right to ask for water wherever they happen to be. So near to the desert that can be a matter of life and death. So I went over to the big-bellied clay jug in which we kept our drinking water. It was next to the gate, half-buried in the sand so that the water would stay cool and fresh. I scooped a beaker full.

"Thank you," said the man who did all the talking. He took a mouthful. "Ah, that's good."

He passed the half-full beaker on to his friends. I could tell by the sweat on their foreheads that the heat was really getting too much for them. "You have very good water in Ngoshe," he said when the beaker was empty. "Are you the one who fetches it from the well in the morning?"

I heard the request behind the question. "Would you like some more?"

He smiled and showed a straight row of bright white teeth. "Of course. If you can spare it."

So I scooped some more water from the clay jug. When I came back to them holding the beaker, I saw that the tall, light-skinned man was looking at me closely. His eye ran over my legs and my hips and rested on the beaker, which I was holding level with my chest. "You're very kind," he said, "and beautiful. What's your name?"

I blushed. "Patience Aiga," I said, telling him my maiden name.

"Patience," he said again. "Patience, my savior, my oasis in the desert . . . "

"Let's not exaggerate!"

"I'm not exaggerating. You've saved us from dying of thirst."

I must admit that I wasn't unhappy about our little exchange. My days were rather monotonous and didn't give me much opportunity to talk to other people. Apart from my relatives and fleeting encounters at the well I hardly saw anybody. So I felt flattered when this attractive man suddenly appeared out of nowhere and started saying all these nice things to me. What was the harm in flirting with him a little?

"And you've come from Gwoza?" I asked him, curious. That was our district capital. It had about fifty thousand inhabitants and lay behind the mountain where we worked our millet field. Seen from the air, the distance was less than three miles. But it was a very difficult journey, because in between there was more than a thousand yards of altitude to cover. And if you took the detour via the road it was just under twenty miles in all.

"Yes," he said. "My name is Ishaku Dabrigela Verhohuna." He held out his hand. I shook it hesitantly, and found myself hoping that my aunt wasn't watching, or anyone else. They might get completely the wrong idea about me.

"I'm a cattle breeder," the man said. "That's why we were here at the cattle market this morning."

"Ah," I said, and tried not to show how impressed I was. "And where are your cattle?"

"I sold them. I got a tidy sum for them."

He was clearly trying to impress me. I liked that. At the same time I was aware that our conversation was drifting into dangerous territory. I shouldn't have been having conversations like this by the door to the yard with a complete stranger. "Well, then I hope you get home safely."

"Yes, of course," he said, and seemed uncertain about whether he should go or not. But anything else would have been very strange. "Thanks again for your hospitality," he said ingratiatingly. "And I hope we will see each other again, beautiful lady."

I hoped so too. After the meeting I was incredibly excited. It was as if lightning had struck in the middle of my dull existence. Suddenly, once again, there was so much more than what had filled my time over the past few months. I wasn't just a maid who did other people's laundry and cooked other people's food. I was a woman, a beautiful woman. And there were people who could see that. Why on earth had I forgotten?

In an instant the dreams that I had buried deep within myself pushed their way violently back to the surface. Why had I believed that my life was over with Yousef's death? Why had I allowed myself to be convinced of that? What if they were all wrong, and I had a future after all? I barely dared to allow myself to think those thoughts. Because as soon as I did I saw myself living the life I had always imagined I would have: as a wife with children running around my feet. And my heart started pounding.

That's enough, I said to myself. Stop that straightaway! I tried to shoo away my fantasies, and instead to concentrate on my household tasks. As a widow you have to be grateful if your uncle takes pity on you. You can't ask too much of life, I heard my mother saying in the back of my mind. Yes, she was right, I found myself thinking: I mustn't neglect my duties and succumb to daydreaming. I hurried to take the laundry off the fence and fold it. Then I lit the fire and began to make dinner. But whatever I did, my thoughts refused to obey. They stayed with him, the tall stranger who had said he thought I was beautiful and he wanted to see me again. Had he been joking, or did he mean it?

I didn't tell anyone in my family about my encounter. I knew instinctively that it was better that way. Luckily no one seemed to have noticed it. At least no one asked me what I'd been talking to the men at the gate about. The day ended, as it always did, with tidying. And the next day began, as it always did, with fetching water. But everything was different:

it was as if yesterday's meeting by the gate had torn away the gray veil that had hung between me and the world since Yousef's death. All of a sudden it seemed brighter and more cheerful.

My friend Rifkatu immediately noticed the change in me. "So, what puts you in such a good mood today?" she asked when we met at the well as usual.

I would have loved to tell her about the man, but I restrained myself. Wouldn't it sound ridiculous for a widow to start talking about butterflies in her belly? Think of your reputation! I reminded myself.

As relaxed and casual as possible, I asked if her relatives in Gwoza had any connections with the Zalidiva tribe.

She looked at me in surprise. "Why do you want to know that?"

"A cousin of mine is interested in one of their girls," I replied.

"Really? Who's the lucky lady?"

"Stupidly I seem to have forgotten her name."

"Then ask," she said. "Then I can make some inquiries. But you generally hear that they are good, Christian people who regularly go to church." She looked at me insistently, as if she could read my mind. "Or are you keeping something from me?"

"Me? What an idea! That's all in the past as far as I'm concerned," I lied, pretending to be highly amused at the idea. Secretly I was wounded by my own words even as I uttered them. But what upset me most of all was that my friend didn't even contradict me.

I performed my daily duties, all the work I generally did, but with more of a spring in my step than usual. As I swept the yard I hummed the song that we had learned in church. That made everything go twice as fast. After that I waited briefly until my aunt and her daughter-in-law, Savan, set off to weed the nearby peanut field. Meanwhile I swept their huts.

Savan's house was full of things that she needed for her baby. She put clean cloths, nappies, cough medicine and creams in a plastic bag. In another she kept her own treasures, mostly things that her husband had given her: fabric to make a new dress, shampoo, a bleaching skin cream, toothpaste, a set of pink underwear and a little mirror. I knew I wasn't allowed to touch those things. But when I saw the mirror I couldn't help myself: I absolutely had to check what I looked like right now.

I hesitantly picked up the mirror and studied my face, something I hadn't done for months. I barely recognized the woman who looked back at me from the glass. She had beautifully shaped brown eyes, a wide nose, high cheekbones and full lips. Was that me? Was I beautiful? I couldn't tell.

I quickly put the mirror away again. What on earth was I thinking? I was making a fool of myself. I hastily went back to work and thanked God that no one had been watching me.

After I had done all my work I didn't really know what to do. To distract myself I went over to my parents' house. My mother was sitting in the shade of a hut, podding beans. I quickly went to give her a hand and kept myself busy like that for a while. But I was getting more and more restless. I caught my thoughts wandering and my eye drifting to the gate.

"Are you waiting for someone?" my mother asked.

"Me? No. Why would I be?"

"You seem so strangely distracted, child."

"No, not at all. It must be the heat."

"Who was that yesterday?"

I gave a start. So my mother, with her keen sense of hearing, had noticed the visit of the men from Gwoza after all. "Just some travelers who wanted a sip of water," I answered truthfully.

"And they didn't want anything else?"

"No."

I left before she could ask me any further questions. My mood darkened once I was back in my uncle's house. It was already afternoon, and the man hadn't turned up. Hour after hour I hoped that he would appear outside the gate as suddenly as he had done the day before. But he didn't.

Eventually I told myself my feelings were ridiculous. Suddenly I was convinced that he wasn't coming anyway and that I had fallen for the compliments of a ladies" man. He had a silver tongue, but he wasn't the savior I had hoped for. He wouldn't free me from my dreary existence as a maid of all work. I had put far too much trust in my encounter with him.

Disappointed, but also furious with myself, I set off to fetch fresh water in the late afternoon. As I was behind schedule, I didn't linger long with the other girls, but hurried back home with the full bucket on my head.

When I turned from the main road into the path that led to our huts, I suddenly saw him: the man from yesterday. He was leaning against the thorn fence of a neighboring farm. He was clearly waiting for me.

My heart nearly stopped.

"I don't suppose I could have a sip of water?" he asked roguishly—with an undertone that suggested we were old accomplices. Why was he so sure of himself? Had I inadvertently given him some sort of sign yesterday? Or did he know that I was a widow? Did that make me easy prey in his eyes?

"I've just come from the well," I said, because I couldn't think of anything better.

"Yes, I know. I've been watching you. All day."

"Really?" I blushed.

"I'll walk you part of the way, OK?"

"No, I'd rather you didn't," I whispered. I looked frantically around to make sure that no one was watching us. "What would people say?"

"Ah, people. I couldn't care less."

"But I could!" I had to think about my family. My father's words came into my head: *Let us pray that she doesn't bring shame upon us.* Was I doing that by talking secretly to Ishaku?

"The only important thing is that you and I understand one another."

"But we don't even know each other!"

"Then it's high time that we got to know each other. Don't you think?"

I was seething inside. On the one hand I was furious about his behavior, on the other I was flattered by it. His wooing words made my heart thump in a way that I had missed so painfully for so long. "You're impossible," I scolded him.

"I can't help it. You're just too beautiful," he insisted.

"Will you be quiet? All the neighbors can hear you! Please go home right now!"

"I'm going. But only if I can see you again tomorrow evening."

My heart leapt. "Fine," I heard myself saying.

"Then until tomorrow evening, at sunset," he said and touched my arm very gently. I felt as if I had been struck by lightning.

Ishaku surprised me several times on the way to the well. He was very nice to me and showered me with compliments. Again and again he said how much he liked seeing my features in the evening light. Sometimes he also brought sweets. I felt very flattered—by his words, and also by the fact that he undertook that difficult journey over the mountain just to see me. I felt pretty in his presence, and very much alive. Over time I became addicted to our moments together, which made me blossom inwardly.

At first the meetings were harmless. But over time Ishaku became more and more insistent and asked me to go with him a little way into the mountains. When no one was looking he touched me in places that he shouldn't really have done. And I found it increasingly difficult to resist his advances. Because my pious principles vanished into air as soon as I was near him. I felt completely infatuated.

I was also aware that I was doing the very thing that my parents had wanted to prevent. But I didn't care. I had a right to live like anyone else, I said to myself defiantly.

When I lay awake at night however, I did start feeling doubts, and I was worried. Did Ishaku know that I was a widow? Was that why he dared to be so forward with me? I was confused about this man—after all, I didn't know much more about him than his name. Because of his age he couldn't be unmarried. What was his life like back in Gwoza? Who were his family?

I didn't dare to ask any of these questions, because I was scared of destroying our happiness. And I didn't want to do that under any circumstances. His presence was too precious to me.


Of course our meetings, which usually took place in public, did not go unnoticed. Neighbors' tongues wagged, and the inevitable happened: eventually my family found out.

I noticed by the way that my uncle's and aunt's faces were darkening from day to day. In the end my father called me to his farm and held me to account. "Who's this man who's chasing you?"

"Which man?"

He slapped my face. "Do you take me for an idiot?" he yelled.

I started crying.

"You know very well who I mean."

"I don't even know him. I've just talked to him a few times."

"Talked," my father repeated sarcastically. "You're making yourself and your whole family a laughingstock, girl. We're a respectable family. There are no whores around here, do you get that?"

Whores! I couldn't believe he had said that word to me. So that was how my own father saw me!

He was absolutely furious. He presented me with a choice: "Either you cut off all contact with this skirt-chaser or you leave your uncle's house right now. And I don't want to see you around here ever again."

"Please forgive me, Father. I'll never meet him again," I said.

After that lecture I felt absolutely terrible. There's nothing worse than losing the respect of your own family. How had I been so thoughtless as to put it at risk? But what hurt me most was the fact that it didn't occur to my father that my relationship with Ishaku might have a future. He couldn't begin to believe that a man would marry a "used model" like myself. That was doubtless how Ishaku saw it as well. I had been incredibly stupid to allow myself to engage in hanky-panky with him, I thought at that moment. Everyone had warned me.

To make quite sure that I didn't do anything stupid again, over the next few days my family wouldn't let me outside the door. I was excused from my daily duty of fetching water until further notice. Instead my aunt sent her daughter-in-law.

Savan, who preferred to sleep in the morning, was in a bad mood about this, and became rather off-hand with me. "A housemaid who has to be protected against herself isn't much help," she said poisonously. "I hope this isn't a permanent state of affairs ... "

"Don't worry," I said. "And I don't much enjoy being your prisoner either."

"Then leave," she sneered. "Find happiness with this man of yours."

I thought it was unbelievably nasty of her to rub salt in my wounds. Because, of course, secretly there was nothing I would have liked more.

After some time, about a week of self-recrimination, something unexpected happened. Suddenly we had visitors: Ishaku and a second man, who I later learned was his brother, stood by the gate of my parents" *kral* in their Sunday best.

No one had expected that. My whole family was thrown into confusion when the two men asked very formally to speak to my father. I watched the whole thing through a gap in the thorn fence that divided the two farms. I thought I was dreaming. Was Ishaku really serious about me? I hadn't even dreamed to imagine as much. But now I was on cloud nine.

When my father led Ishaku across the yard I could tell from his face that he was extremely contented with this development. No wonder, because if Ishaku had actually come to ask for my hand, he had hopes that I might bring in a second bride price. He hadn't expected that.

The men sat down on the tree trunk in front of my father's hut. My uncle and my older brother Yakob joined them. I myself stayed in my hiding place and tried to catch at least a few individual words of their conversation. I was furious that

I couldn't be there myself and had no say in the matter, while they horse-traded over my future. By now Ishaku was bound to have found out that I was a widow. Would it put him off? Or would he be pleased that it gave him the opportunity to lower the price? For some reason I had a feeling that he had known for ages anyway. He had probably made inquiries about me before his visit.

The men talked and talked. From my position behind the fence I could hardly hear a word. I was just struck that my father sounded quite confident. That surprised me. Hadn't he been the one who was always telling me that no man would marry me anyway? Now he seemed to be pretty sure of his case. I hoped devoutly that he wouldn't get carried away and make excessive demands, and send Ishaku running for the hills. After all, my father was aware that this was my only chance. He couldn't afford to be too greedy.

"And how did the discussion go?" I demanded to know when the men had left.

"You're very lucky, girl."

"Did you reach an agreement?"

"He's still thinking."

"What did you ask him for?"

"That's men's business, nothing to do with you."

I later learned from my brother Yakob that my father had demanded a cow and a goat, the normal price. Even I knew that that was excessive for a widow. "Why so much?" I asked furiously. Was he trying to ruin my future?

I asked Yakob to call my father to his senses and bring the price down. But he wouldn't hear of it. "Don't worry," he reassured me. "It will all be fine. Father knows what he's doing."

As I've said, I didn't really understand why my family was so confident. But to my surprise the parties actually reached an agreement. One morning Ishaku's brother brought the animals. That put the seal on the engagement. My family congratulated me. "Now everything will be fine," my mother said.

I was delighted.

At the same time I learned that there would be no wedding feast for me this time. I assumed that this was some kind of economy measure on my father's part. But he assured me that it wasn't customary to have one when a girl was getting married for the second time. "But there will be a church ceremony?" I asked.

"No. No ceremony."

I was very surprised, but I was so happy anyway that I accepted the fact. With or without a ceremony: the main thing was that I was standing on solid ground again. My future was assured.

After that everything went very quickly. My mother and my aunts had already had a range of new dresses made for me: a long skirt, a long-sleeved top and a scarf for my head. It was all made of a purple and green floral fabric. The ensemble wasn't anything like the white ruched wedding dress that I'd worn to my first wedding. Even so I thought it was very pretty.

They washed me, dressed me and called a girl from the village to do my hair. It was very matted, as I had hidden it under my headscarf for the last few months, and hardly combed it. After washing and brushing it she braided it into little plaits that snaked their way across my scalp from my face to the back of my head. I was delighted when she showed me the result in her hand-mirror. I hadn't had such an elegant hairdo for ages.

When everyone thought I looked reasonably presentable, my father called for the ancient Kia that a neighbor of ours used as a taxi. The owner's son was at the wheel. He drove us to my new home; my father, my mother and my uncle came with me as representatives of the family.

I was incredibly excited when we turned into the road for Gwoza. I could hardly believe it: was that really me, sitting dressed like a bride on the backseat of the car?

My mother took my hand. "I don't need to tell you anything about marital duties . . . " she began.

"No, Mother," I cut in, ashamed. We had got that part of things out of the way the first time I got married. I was incredibly embarrassed that she should have brought the subject up again. Did my mother think that just because I had no children she needed to explain the facts of life to me?

"If you have your period, you won't conceive a child," she actually said. "Two weeks later is the best time."

"But I know all that!"

"Fine," she said, and left me in peace for a moment. But she hadn't finished her lecture. "What you should bear in mind: be patient and show humility to the ones who were there before you. Do not engage in arguments. As soon as you have children yourself you will improve your position."

I sat up. Who did she mean? My mother-in-law? "I will treat all his relatives with respect," I promised.

"You must do that, my child. You won't have him to yourself."

"What do you mean by that?"

"Ishaku has married before."

I was thunderstruck. "Is that true?"

"Yes, just like you. But that's unimportant. A hardworking man can feed two families."

All of a sudden it was clear to me: the high bride price that my father had been able to ask for in spite of my widowhood; my family's agreement not to have a church wedding. If you assumed that the marriage was polygamous, suddenly everything made sense. The church fundamentally refused to give such relationships its blessing.

"The pastors have no idea about these things," my mother said, "believe me. Once you've got used to it you'll be glad that you can divide up the housework between yourselves."

My mother carried on giving me advice. But I felt completely powerless and discouraged. It was as if someone had pulled a plug and let all the energy out of my body. I railed against my fate: did the Lord God have it in for me? He was putting me to the test yet again. "Do they have children?" I asked weakly.

"Ishaku and his wife? Yes, of course." She pressed my hand. "But don't let that concern you. You'll give him more. And you'll get on well with the ones he already has."

Then we arrived in Gwoza. The town was considerably bigger and more urban than Ngoshe. Many of the houses in the center were rectangular and built of stone. There were several churches and mosques and even an old hospital built by the missionaries. But on the edges the people lived in round huts, exactly like we did. Many of them kept a few goats that were tied up in front of their houses.

Ishaku's *kral* was right at the foot of the Mandara Mountains. He was waiting for us at the gate. "Welcome!" he called out happily to us.

My husband opened the car door for me and offered me his hand to help me out. If I hadn't just discovered what I had discovered, I might have been delighted and thought of him as a very obliging, respectable man. But now I didn't know what to think of any of that. I saw his three children playing in the yard. Their mother was sitting slightly apart, watching with apparent indifference.

"Good journey?" he asked.

"Yes, thanks," I struggled to say.

"Pull yourself together, Patience," my mother hissed under her breath.

But I couldn't help it. "Is that your wife?" I asked, pointing to the other woman.

"She is my ex-wife, the mother of my children."

He seemed to notice my insecurity and looked deep into my eyes. "You are now my wife, my dearest," he said.

# Getting things wrong

I didn't believe a word Ishaku said. However many times he tried to reassure me on our wedding night in April 2014 that I was his princess and the only woman he loved, it didn't alter the fact that there were three of us in our marriage.

"You should have told me you were already married," I scolded.

"I thought you knew!"

"Not at all! How should I have known?"

We were lying together on my straw mat in the round hut where I was going to live from now on. The hut where Ishaku's wife and the children slept was luckily about ten yards away. I still wondered, of course, whether she was listening in on our nighttime conversation. Like all the men, Ishaku had a roof of his own over his head. But he could visit me whenever he wanted. Or he could visit Lara, his first wife. It was entirely up to him.

"It changes nothing about my feelings for you," he reassured me.

"I believe you, but . . . " But maybe my feelings? And his first wife's?

"You'll get on just fine."

But I wasn't so sure. For my part, at any rate, I could understand Lara not being very keen to share her husband with me. She would probably go around telling all and sundry that I had seduced him. But that didn't seem to worry Ishaku at all.

"You're really ungrateful," he said, disappointed. "I thought you'd be glad you were becoming my wife."

"I am," I assured him. And it was true. In spite of the unexpected circumstances of my marriage, in my emotional chaos at that moment what I felt more than anything was relief. I had left behind the crisis that the death of my first husband had hurled me into. My new position as second wife was better than my previous one as a widow. Even if it meant another woman had to suffer.

"Then I don't want to hear any more. You'll get used to each other," my husband concluded.

We came to terms with each other. I tried to work my way into the everyday life of the family. I knew its rhythms, as they were the same as those in my own family. Like my father and my uncle, Ishaku farmed a millet field in the mountains, which was the source of the family's livelihood. He also owned a few animals: chickens, goats and three cows. His claim to be a cattle-breeder had been a wild overstatement. His wife looked after a garden and a small field of peanuts behind our *kral*.

What I had to offer was my labor. Lara assigned me household tasks. As she was older than me, that was her right, and I had to comply. So I soon found myself performing the same duties as I had at my uncle's house: fetching water in the morning, cleaning the huts and the yard and preparing meals. That took a lot of stress off Lara, and perhaps it was a small compensation for my having landed in the middle of her family. At least that was what I tried to persuade myself.

We didn't talk to each other very much, and if we did it was only ever about practical matters. Did we have enough firewood? Were the animals being fed? Did one of the roofs need to be repaired before the beginning of the rainy season? How many meals would we be able to make with our millet supplies? Did we need extra food from the market?

Lara was neither friendly nor unfriendly to me. She accepted me as a tedious but inevitable evil. Like a relative that you can't choose. And to some extent that was the case. But I knew it wasn't so easy for her to cope with the new situation. Where our intimate life was concerned, Ishaku clearly preferred me, his new, younger wife. At first he visited me almost every night, while Lara lay alone in her hut. He was crazy about me. Of course I liked that.

Sometimes I wondered whether he hadn't even been telling the truth when he described Lara as his "ex-wife": the two of them were an economic unit, but they clearly weren't a loving couple anymore. They were united by the farm, their children and everyday tasks. As his first wife Lara had something like a pension arrangement with my husband.

But the loving couple were Ishaku and me. Even though he often seemed sulky or preoccupied by day, at night he was transformed, he was the lover once more. And I very much enjoyed being the focus of his attention. His nighttime caresses made up for a lot of the things I had to cope with during the day.

His children were a positive surprise to me as well. They were open and unselfconscious with me. They thought my presence in the household as an "aunt" was the most natural thing in the world. The fact that I liked to stir some sugar into our morning *kunnu* also gained me brownie points.

The two boys, Yousufu and Yoshua, were five and seven years old and real rascals: they had so much nonsense in their heads that you could hardly take your eyes off them for a minute. Their little sister Tabita had a calmer temperament, and was much more even-tempered. But she often had to be protected from the attacks of her older brothers. So it was the three-year-old girl that I immediately chose as my favorite among the three. If I had nothing else to do I put her in my lap and just held her there so that she could look at the world around her. She loved that secure spot. And I loved feeling the warmth of that innocent little creature.

But I also had to be careful not to provoke the jealousy of her mother in that respect. Because whenever Lara had a sense that the bond between us was getting too close, she took the little one away from me for the flimsiest of reasons. That hurt me very much. Oh, I thought wearily, how lovely it would be to have a little girl of my own like that. In church on Sunday I prayed to God to grant me fertility.

About church: as a polygamous family we all went there together on Sunday. The first time I was ashamed to appear there as a second wife, since Ishaku and I had not had a Christian wedding. But then I established that there were other families like ours. Even if a man came with two or more wives, he wasn't turned away. No vicar would have dared to refuse a believer the Sunday sermon, and in this way put their soul at stake. But I was refused admission to the choir and the women's association: membership was permitted only to the first wives.

My prayers were heard, and much faster than I had expected. Only a few weeks after my wedding I noticed some physical changes, but thought no further about it.

By now it was May, and we expected the first rain every day; normally it comes in June. But even before that we had our hands full. First we had to dig the fields and loosen the earth. Only then could the soil accept the seed. After the first rainfall it was hardly two days before the seeds began to germinate. From then on we spent every day in the field. The children came with us and helped to defend the precious little plants against the dangerous wild ones.

Weeding was heavy physical work for all of us. Normally I had no problem standing bent over for hours. After all, I had been working in the fields since I was a child. So I was surprised when I suddenly felt ill in the field one morning. I stepped to one side and crouched on the ground to keep from falling over. Then I had to throw up.

Ishaku, who was working not far away, came rushing over. "What is it, Patience?" he asked me. "Are you not feeling well?"

"No," I said weakly.

He held his hand to my forehead. "Do you think you might be ill?"

I listened to my inner voice. "No, I really don't think so."

"You have a rest. Would you like some water?"

"Thanks, I'm fine now," I told him.

I was touched that my husband was so keen to look after me. I sat in the shade of a big tree on the edge of the field for a while and watched the birds in the branches. Then it passed. I went back to the field and started work again. I worked unstintingly until the evening. What had been wrong with me? I wondered—and had no answer.

The next morning we set off at dawn again. It was still quite dark and relatively cool when we took the steep path into the mountains. But soon strangely shaped rocks appeared in the early sunlight. They looked magical. We climbed through them along narrow paths overgrown with thin trees and bushes, to reach our field before the sun was too strong. Ishaku ran ahead as always. Lara and I followed him, as fast as we could with the three children in tow.

I looked into the valley, now lit by the morning sun. Below us lay the town of Gwoza, where I now lived, and from which the whole administrative area took its name. My home village of Ngoshe belonged to the Gwoza district. Soon, when we had reached the highest point, it would be visible on the other side of the mountain range, and I could wave to my mother from the top.

Again I felt nausea welling up in me, but I ignored the feeling, or tried to. Instead I struggled to catch up with Ishaku, who was by now quite far ahead. Then the uneasy feeling in my stomach became so strong that I stopped in the middle of the path. I couldn't walk another step.

"What's up?" I heard Lara saying behind me.

"Nothing. No idea, I just don't feel well."

"Is it what I think it is?"

I looked at her blankly. "What do you think?"

"Well, that you're pregnant?"

The word shot through me like a lightning flash. I felt myself breaking out in a sweat. A moment later I had to throw up again. Lara looked on indifferently.

"What's wrong with her?" asked little Yoshua.

"Nothing serious," his mother reassured him. "She's just a bit weak on her legs."

"What's going on? Are you coming?" Ishaku, who was unaware of all this, called from above.

"Straightaway. We're nearly there," I replied and tried to pull myself together. Even if the suspicion turned out to be true, a pregnancy wasn't a reason for special treatment.

All day in the field I brooded on what Lara had said. She certainly knew more about such things than I did. After all, she had given birth three times. Had she been telling the truth? Or was she making fun of me? She must have known that I was desperately waiting for a child. I prayed to God that she wasn't playing with my emotions.

I secretly felt my belly to check whether she might be right or not. But it was flat as a board. Only my breasts struck me as larger, and they hurt. Did that mean anything? I didn't know. I barely dared to hope that it actually might be so. Unfortunately I didn't have a female confidante in Gwoza who I could have asked. And though my mother lived only a couple of miles away, it was still too far to ask for advice.

My husband was the only one I felt close to in my immediate surroundings. When he visited me in my hut in the evening I could no longer hold back and told him about Lara's suspicions. He wasn't very surprised.

"Do you think she might be right?" I asked.

"Why not? I'm very fertile," Ishaku boasted. He put his ear to my belly and pretended to listen. "Hello!" he called. "Anyone in there?" He laughed. I laughed too. But in fact it was quite a serious matter for me, and I needed certainty about it.

"Should we send for Saratu?" I suggested. She was an elderly woman who knew about herbs. She was also brought in to deal with childbirth.

"Not at all," he said. "She always wants money."

I pulled a disappointed face. I was already annoyed with myself for even confiding in him.

"At least you're not ill," he carried on. "And if there is a child growing in your belly we'll get to see it soon enough."

The morning sickness came and went. Most days I was fine. Then others would come when I was very ill. Lara looked at me knowingly when the attacks came. There were lots of things I would have liked to ask her, but I held back. We weren't all that close, after all. Instead I decided to talk to my mother about it as soon as possible.

I could hardly wait. It would be wonderful to know that a son or daughter was on the way, a child that would give my own existence a new meaning.

But first I had to be patient. Because at the moment we had so much work that there was no time for family visits. We exhausted ourselves in the fields from dawn till dusk.

I was very glad that at least there was no need to fetch water every morning during the rainy season. We caught the water from the roofs of the huts in big plastic sheets and filled whole canisters with it. But I still had to make breakfast for everyone. And the evening meal was my responsibility as well. So in the afternoon I always came back a little earlier than the others, because after the work in the fields everyone was starving. The children complained if there wasn't something hot to eat as soon as they got home, so I always tried to make sure the food was ready on time.

One evening I heard my family coming back to the compound with the neighbors. But even before I saw them I was aware that the mood had changed. The usual hubbub of voices and laughter was missing. Even the children weren't making the racket that they normally did when they got back. Instead of staying to chat, the people said goodbye and hurried to their respective compounds.

I opened the gate for the homecomers. The children were the first to slip inside. Then came Lara, and Ishaku last of all. "What's up?" I asked when he stepped into the yard. "Has something happened?"

He seemed relieved to see me. "I'm glad you're home," he said, and hugged me. He usually never did that in front of the others.

"Yes, of course." Where else would I have been?

"Did you have any problems on the way home?"

"No." I walked along that path every day.

"Did you meet anyone?"

I shook my head.

"Boko Haram are supposed to be in the area . . ."

"Here, in Gwoza?"

I looked at Ishaku in horror. And as if by some kind of trick I suddenly saw not him, but my first husband, lying stiff and lifeless in a pool of blood on the floor. The past that I had wanted to forget had forced its way violently back into the present, and I immediately felt an urge to run away. I knew these murderers. I started to shiver. "Where are they?" I asked in alarm. "Are they somewhere around here?"

"We came across some people in Ngoshe who had run away from them."

From Ngoshe—my home village. "For heaven's sake!" I said. "What's happened there?"

"Boko Haram raided the village. That's what people are saying."

What about my family? Were they safe? "Did you ask them after my parents?"

"Yes, of course. But they didn't know anything about them. Some of the villagers were working in the fields when they came. The rest hid or ran away or . . ."

Yes, I thought, but my mother, who usually stayed at home because she was blind, couldn't run away if there was no one there to take her by the hand. That would have been my task. I felt very guilty for not having been there for her.

"We need to go and check on them!"

"Are you crazy? Now that it's getting dark it would be far too dangerous to set off on the road."

Ishaku was right. After all, no one knew where the Boko Haram fighters would be after their raid. But they were probably still somewhere nearby. So it was quite possible that we would run right into their arms. I didn't want to risk that. "Then at least try to contact my uncle."

Ishaku took out his phone and dialed the number, but the line was dead. "They've probably blown up the towers so that we can't contact each other," he guessed, and tried to call his sister who lived in another village, but he couldn't get through to her either. "It seems to affect the whole Gwoza district," he said, and thoughtfully scratched his head. "I'd like to know what plans they have for this area."

Now I started to become really frightened. What did Ishaku mean by that? His remark shook the image of Boko Haram that I'd previously had in my mind.

Until now I had seen my husband's murderers as an Islamist gang that hunted down Christians or Christian institutions. Relatively often you heard of them killing Christians in the immediate surroundings or further away, setting a church on fire or attacking a school. The abduction of over two hundred schoolgirls from Chibok, a village the size of Ngoshe, had attracted a lot of attention in the spring. Everyone suspected that the girls were being held in the nearby Sambisa Forest, to which the group often withdrew.

But in most cases it was influential individuals that were attacked by Muslim radicals. People Boko Haram thought disadvantaged the Muslim population. The Yousefs, my first husband's family, were typical in that respect. Such punishment actions were designed to intimidate other Christians and drive them out of the region. But Muslims who didn't agree with their warped worldview were shot down as well: only recently we had buried the emir of Gwoza, Alhaji Idrissa Timta.

But I had never heard of the sect trying to conquer a whole territory for itself. That was why I was unsettled by Ishaku's turn of phrase. Had he told me everything he knew? "What else did the people from Ngoshe tell you?" I asked him nervously.

He looked at the ground. "It was a very big and well-planned attack," he said. "The Boko Haram people came on motorbikes. They are supposed to have fallen on the village like an army."

I felt very miserable. "Were many people killed?" I whispered.

"Probably. No one knows exactly."

That evening I couldn't face eating or doing anything else sensible. I was constantly thinking about my family. I sat dully in front of my hut staring into the middle distance, until eventually Ishaku told me to join him in bed and sleep a little. But I couldn't sleep a wink. Not before I had some idea of what had happened to my parents and my brothers and sisters.

"They probably ran up to their field like all the other villagers and we'll find them there tomorrow morning," he said, trying to reassure me.

"Yes," I replied. "I hope so." But I was still uneasy. I guessed that something terrible had happened.

I spent all that night in Ishaku's arms, listening to his heartbeat and breathing in the smell of his body. He was strong, and would protect me if necessary. I loved that man. And I needed him, and so did the baby growing in my body. Ishaku wouldn't abandon me as my first husband had done. He would stay with us and look after us.

The next morning I got dressed, hastily made breakfast and couldn't wait to get going. First of all, as usual, we set off along the steep path that led to our field on the mountain. Lara stayed there with the children, weeding as they did every day.

The other side led down to the valley. That was the most direct and the shortest way to Ngoshe, even if it wasn't actually a path, more a battle through bushes and rocks. But at that precise moment no one dared to use the actual road. It was simply too dangerous, because no one knew where the Boko Haram people were.

Among the bushes and the big boulders that lay around everywhere on the slope, we met some people from Ngoshe who had spent the night up here. Their fear was still etched on their faces. Yes, they confirmed, the attackers had come to the village on motorbikes, in large numbers. They had claimed to be a unit of the Nigerian army, and as they were all wearing military uniforms, the villagers believed them. They thought the army wanted to protect the area against Boko Haram, because too many Christians lived there. But then the men went from one farm to another and asked where the Christians lived. Shots were heard, and screams.

"Then I picked up my two grandchildren and ran as fast as I could," said an old man with two boys. I knew him very well, as he lived near my parents.

"Have you seen my father or my uncle?" I asked him.

"No, my child." He noticed my anxious face. "But that doesn't mean anything."

"Some men who were up here during the night," someone else said, "went back to the village early this morning."

"That's where we wanted to go too."

The old man looked doubtful. "I don't understand why everyone's in such a hurry," he said.

"What do you mean?"

"Who knows if those people are still somewhere nearby ... Do what you think is right. But I'm staying here with my grandchildren for the time being. I'm responsible for them."

His words made me think. Would Ishaku and I be putting ourselves in danger if we went down to the valley now? At any rate we were taking a risk. It would probably have been more sensible not to go. On the other hand I also felt responsibility toward my family. I was out of my mind with worry about them.

Ishaku sensed that. "I suggest the following," he said. "Let's make our way down there very slowly and turn round immediately if anything seems at all strange. What do you think?"

I said I agreed.

"Good luck!" the old man called after us. "I hope you find your parents!"

We climbed further downhill along the paths that led between the bushes and boulders. Then we left the shelter of the undergrowth. There was a ghostly silence as we approached the settlement. A smell of burnt straw hung in the air. I could see that some of the roofs of the round huts were charred. Boko Haram had clearly set them on fire. But in the rainy season millet straw didn't burn particularly well. Had they created havoc in my parents' farm or my uncle's?

We approached the *kral*. That curious silence again. There was no one but us in the street. All the people who had stayed in the village or come back to it were hiding in their farms. I saw two human bodies lying at the end of the path. I felt an impulse to hurry over to them. But then I became aware of the sickly, rotten smell that was coming from them. I was terrified when I realized that they were corpses. Ishaku held me tightly by the hand.

"We should get back," he said. But by now we were only a little way from my family's farm.

"Let me just check on them quickly."

"All right then," he said rather reluctantly. "But then we should get out of here."

Ishaku walked with me to the gate and we stepped into the farmyard. I found my family gathered there: my father, my uncle, my aunt and one of my brothers. But then I was struck by their frozen faces. They were standing in a circle around a hole which—probably in great haste—they had dug beside the thorn fence. They didn't say a word when I walked over to them. They didn't need to. Strangely, I knew exactly what was happening here. I barely dared to look into the hole.

Yes, there she lay, my dear mother. She was wrapped in a white cloth with a big red stain level with her chest. Her eyes were closed for ever.

I felt a sense of utter despair when I saw her like that. My mother! Why had they focused their rage on my poor, sick mother? And since when had this sect murdered defenseless women? Women who had never done anything to them did not deserve such a death.

Suddenly I felt utterly alone within my family circle. I was the loneliest person in the world. Tears sprang into my eyes, but I couldn't cry.

"What happened?" I asked my father.

"We found her not far from the church. She couldn't get to safety quickly enough," he said. It sounded almost like an apology. Of course, while the attack was actually going on it wouldn't have occurred to anyone to look for my mother. Their first instincts had been to get themselves to safety.

I didn't reproach them for it. If I blamed anyone it was myself for leaving her on her own. If I hadn't recently got married and moved away I would have been able to protect her. I would have taken her by the hand and gone with her into the mountains. Then she wouldn't have been lying life-less in that damp hole.

My father drew the cloth over my mother's face. He hur-riedly said the Lord's Prayer. Then he began to cover the corpse with soil. I had to turn away because I couldn't bear the sight of it. How could it be that the people close to me were being slaughtered while I went on living?

"Forgive me, Mother," I whispered. "Forgive me for not being able to do anything for you."

Ishaku helped the other men to fill the hole. Then he called for us to hurry. "We shouldn't stay here any longer than necessary," he said to me. "It's not over yet."

"You think they'll come back?"

"I'm not a clairvoyant. But it's better not to run the risk."

So we climbed back up the mountain. My father, my brother, my uncle and my aunt came too. They wanted to camp out near the field for a while and they brought with them all the food supplies that they still owned at that time of year, to hide them up in the mountains, because there had also been looting in the neighborhood.

"We'll be safer in the mountains," my father said. "Sometimes I wonder if we wouldn't have been better off never leaving them."

That was an old debate in the villages, which reared its head every time there was a crisis. Whether our lives were made difficult by a bad orange harvest, a dried-up well or arguments with the Fulani nomads, the valley-dwellers always asked themselves the same question: hadn't the life that the tribe had led up in the mountains until the middle of the previous century been better than our lives were now? Had it been the right thing to follow the call of the missionaries and cultivate the valley?

If they had decided otherwise back then, much in our present situation would have been simpler. On the one hand we wouldn't have had quarrels with our Muslim neighbors—and no one would have sympathized with Boko Haram just to settle a score with us. On the other hand, up there we would have been much better protected against attacks. For the older generation it was still a well-practiced tradition to seek refuge in the mountains. So I wasn't surprised by my father's decision. Soon more villagers were bound to follow.

And then I thought of us, of Ishaku's family, mine and Lara's. Yesterday the attackers had been in Ngoshe, carrying out a massacre. But who could guarantee that they wouldn't find their way to Gwoza tomorrow? The district capital, with a majority Christian population, was only a stone's throw away on the other side of the mountain. And there too, there were Boko Haram sympathizers. We knew that from their attacks on individuals. Perhaps they would soon be hosting bloodbaths like the one in Ngoshe?

"I think they want to drive us out of the whole region," I said to Ishaku, as we walked through the undergrowth.

"Yes, it's very worrying," he agreed. "They're active all over the whole Gwoza district now. What happened in Ngoshe yesterday probably happened in other villages at the same time. Something's brewing."

His words made me even more anxious. "Don't you think we should get out of here?" I asked him.

He laughed. "Where do you want to go, excuse me?"

"I don't care. Anywhere. Maybe Cameroon." The border was only about six miles away.

"Fine, then, Cameroon." Ishaku repeated the name of the country as if I'd been coming out with a lot of nonsense. "And where are we going to live?"

"I don't know," I admitted. "We can sell the goats. I mean . . . It would only be temporary."

"Are you trying to ruin me? I have three children to feed!"

Four! I wanted to correct him: he had clearly forgotten already that I was expecting a child as well. But I choked the words back. There was no point arguing with him. We were both tense enough.

"You should at least think for the sake of your children," I said in a conciliatory voice.

He said nothing, and actually seemed to be brooding on the subject for a moment. "You know that's not possible," he said. "Not during the rainy season. We can't just leave the millet in the field."

"What about after the harvest?"

"If the situation hasn't improved."

I could see that he was right. We simply couldn't afford to abandon the harvest. Our families would starve, and I didn't want that. So I agreed with him that for now we would continue as before. In the evening I knelt on my straw mat and folded my hands to have a conversation with God. I wanted to ask him for protection. As the army and the state administration were both failing, I was convinced that he alone could help us drive Boko Haram out of the region. "Now those animals have taken two beloved people away from me," I told him. "Was that a test? If so, that's enough. I can't take any more."

Over the next few days more and more terrible details came to light about the massacre that had taken place on June 2, 2014, in the villages of Ngoshe, Attagara, Agapalwa and Aganjara. We learned that on that day several hundred people had been killed. The male inhabitants in particular had been systematically slaughtered. The ones who had tried to escape by the main road had been intercepted by motorcyclists. Children had been torn from their mothers" arms and shot.

I was shocked when people told me these details. If I hadn't seen the dead in Ngoshe with my own eyes, I would have found it hard to believe that the group was capable of cruelties on such a scale.

People said it might have something to do with the fact that the Sambisa Forest was getting too small as a place of retreat. Boko Haram had recently grown considerably. Many Muslims who were dissatisfied with the central government and wanted more autonomy for the Muslim population in the north were joining of their own free will. Others were forced into it. When the sect members stood at the door with machetes they had no choice but to pretend solidarity with the group. At any rate they were constantly growing in number.

And they no longer lived in the shadows as they had done in the early years. What had previously been a secret association was developing more and more into an army of militiamen. Their members had to be given food and board. So they were carrying out more and more robberies and plundering raids.

Given this development it would have been only logical for them to demand their own territory: a place to which their fighters could retreat if they weren't actually fighting—and one that might be a bit more pleasant and accessible than the mosquito- and malaria-infested Sambisa swamps. Had they chosen our home for that purpose? Did they want to grab the villages of the Gwoza district and drive us all out? Or kill us? Or what exactly did they plan for us?

Of course our neighbors in the district capital were worried about events as well. Relations between Muslims and Christians here were more tense than they had ever been. It made us Christians furious that the Muslims were so passive, and didn't speak out more clearly against the group's atrocities. They were our neighbors, after all! Why weren't they standing by us? Did they secretly support the goal of driving us away? Or were they afraid of revenge attacks? We didn't know who to trust in this situation.

The next three weeks passed uneventfully. My family and I stuck to our regular rhythm: we set off at the crack of dawn to spend the day in the field, and in the early afternoon I always came down a little earlier than the others to the *kral* to make dinner for everyone. Then we ate together, did the work that needed doing around the farm and let the day slowly fade.

By now we were a highly effective team. Quite honestly, at first I couldn't have imagined that this three-partner marriage would have worked so well. But I must admit that in terms of labor organization it had its advantages. And where the other aspects of marriage were concerned, Lara was hardly competition for me; at night I had Ishaku to myself, and enjoyed his undivided attention. So in spite of all the uncertainties and the adverse circumstances in which we found ourselves, I was happy in my new marriage: I had found my place. And once I had had a baby, my membership in the family would no longer be negotiable, I knew that.

When I trudged back down to the valley as usual on the afternoon of June 23, I was in a good mood. I was wondering how long it would take for my belly to swell and make my condition apparent to everyone, particularly to Ishaku. As far as I knew it would be months before other people saw anything.

Once I got home I filled a big pot with water, stacked the firewood and lit the flames between the three cooking stones. While I was looking for some ingredients to make the millet broth a little tastier, I hummed a hymn that I particularly liked. It had been buzzing around in my head.

Then suddenly I heard the rattle of engines and shots nearby. My heart froze. Was it what I feared? Had they come to Gwoza? "Please God, don't let it be true," I prayed.

I doused the flames and looked around to see where I could hide. "*Allahu Akbar*," I heard the men shouting outside. They were already pushing open the door to our farm and storming in.

"Where is the infidel who owns this *kral*?" they asked me, pointing their guns at me; maybe our neighbors had told them we were Christian. "Where is your husband?"

"I have no husband," I lied, because I knew that they always killed the men first. That was what they had done in Ngoshe, after all. "I am unmarried."

"All the better," they laughed. "Then we'll improve your luck a bit!"

"No!" I cried.

"Don't argue." Two of the armed men held me by the arms. I lashed out and kicked around me.

I watched them taking all the food supplies from our hut and carrying them away. They untied the animals too. "Have you any more hidden away?"

"No," I insisted. "These are all we have."

"Then off we go. You're coming with us."

"Have pity on me!" I pleaded.

But they dragged me away.

# Women as spoils of war

Sitting on the bench in front of me is a middle-aged woman with jet-black eyes, her full face framed in an Islamic head-scarf. There are dark horizontal stripes on her forehead and cheeks. She was tattooed with the signs of her tribe during an initiation ritual when she was a teenager.

That's an old local tradition, and there are historical reasons for it. It meant that a girl's membership of a tribe was visible even if she was abducted by other tribes. You hardly ever see women with tattooed faces anymore. The practice fell out of fashion once the age of women's abduction seemed to have come to an end. "We had no idea that the subject would one day be current again," the woman says with a sigh.

No one knows the topic better than she does. Asabe Kwambula is headmistress of the school from which the Chibok girls were kidnapped in April 2014. Since the school-girls disappeared, she has been fighting for their release. But

Asabe has a hard task ahead of her: the guards on the gate don't want to let her into the church compound. Unlike many of her pupils, the headmistress is an adherent of the Muslim faith, and is dressed accordingly. She wears a black veil with white dots, though she hasn't covered her face.

I have been in contact with Asabe ever since her pupils were abducted. I have called her many times from Germany and asked her how the search was going. She was rarely able to tell me good news. For a long time the army's efforts seemed fruitless. Several times she was asked to identify girls who had been freed. But none of her pupils was ever among them. The first "real" Chibok girl wasn't to reappear until the spring of 2016.

Meanwhile Asabe herself—like so many of the people of Chibok—has become a refugee. She now lives in Maiduguri. Even though she's a Muslim, living in Chibok became too dangerous for her. She has come to the church because I asked her for an interview. She agreed straightaway to meet me in the grounds of the EYN church, and wasn't worried about coming into contact with the other religion. "That's not an issue: here some people believe this, others that," she claims and tells me that her nephew is getting married in this church on Saturday. She has been invited to the wedding. "Families here are a mixture of religions, no one wants to do anything bad to anyone else."

But when you see the dark looks that the Christians in the compound give her, you get another impression. The Muslim headmistress is fighting against a wave of suspicion. People know her. "What's she doing here?" they ask behind their hands.

Many members of the Christian community in Maiduguri think Asabe Kwambula gave tacit agreement to the abduction of the schoolgirls, or was at least informed in advance. Why else was she the only one to urge that they take their school leaving exam when the governor of Borno had already called for all activities at schools in his jurisdiction to be postponed to the next school year for safety reasons? And why did she happen to be away on the night of the attack?

"That's absolute nonsense," she says stoutly. "I'm a victim of this crime myself. I've been driven from my home too, as have many of my Muslim neighbors."

She insists that she thinks day and night about the girls. Sometimes she dreams about them. "They've become a security pledge of the war raging between the Islamists and Nigeria's central government," she explains. There is responsibility on both sides: "As women here are traditionally seen as the 'possessions' of men, in cases of conflict, they try to take them away from their opponent in order to weaken him."

She is referring to the fact that Boko Haram and its leader Shekau only allowed the mass abduction of girls and women after a particular event: when Shekau's own wife and his three children had been taken prisoner by the army.

That happened in September 2012. Shekau and his family were attending a naming ceremony with relatives near Maiduguri. That ceremony is very important in Africa, and is celebrated accordingly. However the Nigerian army had got wind of the event. Dozens of soldiers burst in on the party and opened fire on the guests. Shekau was shot in the thigh. Even though he was badly injured, he managed to flee. But the soldiers took his wife and children into custody. They are still behind bars even today.

That was a great defeat for Shekau, both a hard personal blow and an insult to his pride as an African and a Muslim man. With the "theft" of his wife and children he had been profoundly humiliated, particularly in the eyes of his own men, who—encouraged by Salafist preachers—have an extremely conservative view of women. According to this, it is the supreme duty of a man to protect his wife against other men. If he doesn't manage to do so, both of them are dishonored. Shekau couldn't put up with that. To restore his reputation and win back respect, there was only one possible option: revenge.

A little later Shekau published a video. The film shows him sitting in his tent in some unknown town, holding his Kalashnikov. He announces in the plainest terms that he will take revenge for the theft of his wife: "Wait and see what will happen to your wives according to sharia law," he says. Even then the message made me shudder. It was unmistakable: Shekau was telling his opponents that he was going to attack their women too. In a later address he even threatened the president directly: "I will take Jonathan's daughter prisoner . . . I would like you to know that there is slavery in Islam: even during the battle of Badr the Prophet Muhammad took slaves."

And he was as good as his word. A year later he abducted the Chibok schoolgirls. But that event, which was reported in the world's media, only represents the sad climax of an incredible series of kidnappings. Several thousand women and girls are believed to be in the hands of the terrorists by now. While the West concentrates on the fate of the Chibok girls, it is largely ignored that their abduction is not the exception but the rule—as the sad fate of Patience indicates.

In conversation with Asabe I come to understand the principle of the radical Islamist campaign more and more clearly. The women and girls are the currency with which Shekau buys the loyalty of his followers. In a country in which many young men have no work and therefore cannot get married, the prospect of a bride as the spoils of war is highly enticing. It is seen as one of the main attractions of the sect, which— unlike ISIS—does not pay its fighters decent wages: Shekau baits the young men with, among other things, the promise of sex.

The sexual slavery that he imposes on these women is also a program of religious cleansing. For the soldiers, the forced "weddings" go hand in hand with the exhortation to produce offspring: Muslim offspring, of course. In the worldview of the Islamists the father is crucial, and all children produced from such unions are automatically considered to be Muslims. The woman who carries the pregnancy to term serves only as fertile ground in which the warrior's seed can flourish. But in order to ensure a Muslim upbringing for her Boko Haram children, it is seen as desirable for her to learn the Qur'an before the "wedding" and convert to Islam.

"I'm almost sure that my pupils have all been forced into marriage by now, and that they will all have had babies," the headmistress says sadly, with a note of frustration.

Asabe is under no illusions—and she won't let me have

any either: the long-term goal of Boko Haram, I understand, is nothing but the extermination of all Christians and infidels in the north of Nigeria. The kidnapped girls who have been forced into marriage also have the task of producing more Muslim children with their tormentors. In its boundless chauvinism the sect sees the girls' bodies only as incubators for their own reproduction.

# Kidnapped

The Boko Haram fighters were rampaging everywhere in the neighboring area. They had come in their dozens, and fallen on Gwoza like a swarm of plundering ants.

When they took me to the gate, I heard them shouting *"Allahu Akbar"*; shouts and shots reached me from the other huts. They were dragging out big sacks of millet and rice as well as other supplies of food, and bringing them to their motorbikes, three-wheelers and pickups parked on the main road. I saw the cattle being driven there from the other farms. Then came the women and children. They simply shot a lot of the men when they got in their way.

"Come on, tell us which houses the Christians live in," said the two men who had grabbed me by the arms and were pulling me toward the vehicles. "Tell us where they're hiding."

"I don't know."

"We might let you go if you tell us."

"But I really have no idea!" I insisted. They jabbed their rifle butts into my side. I bent double with pain. Of course I couldn't help thinking of my baby. Should I tell them I was pregnant? But an inner voice persuaded me otherwise.

"You'll regret it if you don't help us," they told me. "But it doesn't matter. We'll smoke you out somehow. No infidel will be left alive in Gwoza."

Their words terrified me. What I would have given at that moment to warn Ishaku somehow, so that he wouldn't come down from the mountain and run straight into their arms. Since he was a man, they would make short work of him. But there was nothing I could do.

They forced me onto the flatbed of a motorized three-wheeler. It was already crammed with other frightened women, Christians like me. I recognized one of them as my neighbor Jara. We stood closely together. We were guarded by a Boko Haram man with a Kalashnikov around his neck. Meanwhile the others loaded their loot onto the pickups: grain, goats and the straw that they had stripped from the roofs. They took everything that might be useful to them. And we were clearly part of their booty.

My heart thumped wildly when the engine started. The smell of petrol filled my nostrils. Was there any chance of fleeing? I wondered. Could I jump off the car? I took an uncertain step forward. But the guard immediately saw what I was planning.

"Hey, you," he said to me, "don't even think about it!" He tied my wrists together with a rope, and tied the other women up in a similar way. And finally he bound us all together so that none of us could move without taking the others with us.

So there we all stood with our hands bound, each of us more fearful than the other. "I've heard that they don't hurt women," Jara said, perhaps to reassure herself.

"Really? So where are they taking us?"

"They're going to kill us. They kill all the Christians," wept a young girl standing next to me.

"Nonsense! They could have killed us here," I told her. I don't know why I was so certain about it. Perhaps it had something to do with the fact that I had already seen how few qualms the Boko Haram people had about committing murder if that was what they wanted to do. So if they didn't, there must have been a reason for it. They had other plans for us.

"But what do they want from us?" the girl asked.

"I don't know," I shouted at her. Her questions were driving me crazy.

Our three-wheel truck rumbled through the streets of Gwoza. We desperately scanned our surroundings for any family members. Someone who might be able to stop us from being kidnapped. But there was no one who would have been capable of it. All the Christian residents of Gwoza who hadn't been cut down by Boko Haram were in hiding somewhere.

We left the town in a column. We turned northward into the cross-country road, the A13, the main connecting route between Mubi in the south and Maiduguri in the north—the road that the inhabitants of the Gwoza district no longer dared to use because it was said to have fallen into the hands of the terrorists.

We drove beneath the extensive mountain range and passed the village of Warable. Then we reached Pulka, where the mountains flattened out on our right. The column of terror drove confidently into the village. In Pulka the roads were eerily empty. No one dared to come out of their houses.

At the crossroads we turned east. My heart almost stopped: this was the way to my parents' house. Where were they taking us? Were we on the way to my old home of Ngoshe? At first I didn't know whether to think that was good or bad. In Ngoshe someone might be able to help me, I thought. Then I became terrified: it would be a death sentence for my family if the terrorists had chosen Ngoshe as their new base.

"Dear God, let it be somewhere else!" I prayed.

We actually drove past the road that led to my home village and continued on toward the east. The road led through fields that were unusually green at that time of year. The millet stalks were already very tall. But here and there a tree loomed above the plants. Soon, I thought, we should reach the river that formed the border with the neighboring country of Cameroon. It was only a few miles away from Ngoshe toward the east.

We passed through Ashigashiya, a sleepy border town. I knew it from before, as I had been there a few times. My family had relatives here. My father's oldest brother, Uncle Amadou, lived in Ashigashiya with his family, but we weren't in contact with him very much.

The little towns seemed different. I was struck at first by

the fact that black flags flew on several of the roofs, a sign that the inhabitants sympathized with Boko Haram. For heaven's sake, I thought: so they publicly supported the terrorists. Did the Muslim inhabitants of the town do that of their own free will? Or had they been forced? Was it a way of protecting themselves against attacks? But it wasn't easy to grasp what was happening here just by looking. Perhaps everyone who had stayed had switched sides and now belonged to Boko Haram.

Just before the end of the village we turned into the entrance to a house built of wood and stone. It might have been the mayor's house, or an administrative building that had something to do with the nearby border. In the courtyard there was a loud hubbub in the gathering darkness. Men in military uniforms and with Islamic caps on their heads were busy shooing civilians into the house.

"Get out!" the man who had been guarding us during the journey commanded. But he made no sign of untying us. "Get out! Nearly done!" he repeated.

We struggled down from the bed of the truck. "Right, now in there," he said and pointed to the house into which the other prisoners were disappearing too.

"What are we doing here?" a woman asked.

No one replied.

"At least untie us, or we won't be able to move!"

The man did just that. Then he shoved us roughly inside the building. We stumbled into a room that was already full of people: a few men and lots of women and children, none of whom seemed to have realized that they had become the booty of the terrorists. They looked completely scared and confused. Guards carrying machetes and Kalashnikovs stood at the door and the windows. The atmosphere was oppressive, the air stale. And of course we were terribly afraid of what would happen next. Perhaps the uncertainty was the worst.

"Maybe they do want to shoot us," I whispered to Jara, who was crouching nearby.

She too was uncertain now, but she clung to her hope. "I think they have other plans for us."

It was slowly growing dark outside. In the courtyard I heard the Boko Haram people's evening prayer. What a strange god they were praying to, I thought. What god demands of his congregation that they kill other people or take them prisoner? Was it the same god that our Muslim neighbors prayed to? They had never behaved like that to us, and never mentioned that anyone demanded they do so. Although I didn't know much about these matters, I suspected that these men were making a terrible mistake. Someone must have poisoned their thoughts. Perhaps they had been put under a spell. That happens relatively often here.

How were things at home? Had Ishaku, Lara and the children come back from the mountains? I should have warned them somehow. I felt terribly guilty, but I couldn't think of a way to do it. "At least see to it that they noticed early enough and stayed up there," I prayed to my God. "Protect my husband, please don't let me be a widow again." In spite of the wretched situation in which I found myself, that was my biggest fear: that my husband would be stolen from me again. Particularly now that I hoped to bring his child into the world. I didn't want it growing up without the protection of a father.

We sat there in the room for a long time and waited, but nothing happened. Some of the other prisoners sat dozing. I leaned back to back with one of the women who had come with me from Gwoza. I didn't know her, but the fact that we came from the same town somehow gave us a bond here, far from home.

I don't know how long we spent sitting on the floor. Eventually the smell of cooked meat reached me from outside. I heard the clatter of plates and voices. Our kidnappers were clearly having their dinner. I felt hungry too, and thirsty. But of course in our prison we got nothing. It was as if we didn't even exist for these men. After a while I almost believed they'd forgotten us.

That might even have been the best thing: if they just forgot us and went on another raid the next morning, so that we could escape in the meantime. Amid those nonsensical hopes I eventually fell into exhausted sleep.

I woke when the cocks in the village started crowing. It was still dark. At first I didn't know where I was: as I did every morning, I felt the impulse to go out and fetch water from the well. But then, in the gloom, I became aware of all the bodies around me. I saw the shadowy faces of the people and heard their breathing. Some slept, others stared into the distance. After that night the bodies and the air smelled very strongly in the room. Some of us had probably relieved ourselves on the spot, because there was nothing else to be done.

I began to panic: no, yesterday had not been a bad dream. I was in the middle of a nightmare. Perhaps it had only just begun. How long would we be crammed together in this stinking room?

Outside the call of the muezzin rang out, and we heard the men in the yard praying. Then all of a sudden the door burst open. They waved their Kalashnikovs and machetes. "Right, that's enough lazing about," they said. "Out you come!"

We looked at each other, confused. Were they letting us go?

"Right, come on! Hurry up!" they roared and pushed us toward the exit. If someone went on sitting on the floor or didn't move quickly enough, they beat them. The children began to cry. I didn't know what to make of this action. But anything was better than just staying in that room. So I allowed them to push me to the door.

I blinked when I stepped outside. The morning sun shone into my face. Feeling its warm beams on my skin gave me a curiously comforting feeling. They were like a sign from my God, saying to me: "Here I am! I haven't abandoned you!" At least that was how it felt to me.

Then we were all standing in the yard, several dozen people. It was hard to believe that we had all fitted into that room. The fighters arrived in front of us with cheeky grins on their faces. They apparently enjoyed having so much power over us. Frightened, my fellow prisoners and I stared at the barrels of the rifles pointing at us. None of us knew what their plans were for us. But I could read it in the faces of the others: a lot of them thought they were going to shoot us down now. I pushed myself into the back row near the wall of the building. For some reason I thought it would be better if our tormentors didn't have us right in their field of vision.

Most of them were very young, but there were some older men too. They all wore curious homemade uniforms, such as a pair of military trousers with a camouflage pattern, trainers and a T-shirt. Some of their outfits looked quite tattered. You could tell that some had recently led a different life: they were fatter, and wore superior clothing. Clearly they had only joined Boko Haram quite recently.

Then a middle-aged man with a black beard and a woollen cap came on to the scene. Their leader? He wore a strange expression on his face: half devilish, half stupid, full of contempt. Later I found out that I had probably met the supreme leader of Boko Haram.

But apart from his facial expression, nothing about him distinguished him much from the other men in the group. He too wore a random collection of military clothing. A machine gun dangled around his neck, along with several magazines of cartridges, which gave him a particularly warlike appearance. The others treated him like a tribal leader, with the greatest possible respect.

"We are the warriors of the true belief," he said, staring at us. "The belief in the one true God, Allah." He threw his arms into the sky, as if to draw strength from it. But then he suddenly spat: "Cursed be those of you who have betrayed and sold him!"

He looked grimly around. "The north of Nigeria has

always been the land of Muslims. But then the white missionaries came to lead us astray. They planted their false beliefs in
people's heads. Many stayed on the right path. But some were
too weak; you were too weak—you have denied the true god,
because you hoped for advantages from that denial. You have
allowed yourselves to be abused by the white people. And
they had only one goal: to make Muslims slaves in our own
country and drive us away from here. Shame on all those
who helped them!"

The man had talked himself into a fury. Now he actually
looked quite insane. I could clearly see that his own men
were very afraid of him. Nonetheless they hung on his words,
and seemed to be entirely under his spell.

"But let us turn the tables," he roared. "We will win back
our country for the Muslims to whom it really belongs. We will
cleanse it and purify it of all infidel elements. The rule of the
earthly powers over northern Nigeria is a thing of the past."

The man took a deep breath. "My people and I will not rest
before we have eradicated all godless people. We will have no
pity on the traitors. But you have the choice. You can decide
which side you want to stand on in this battle: on the side of
the true believers or on the side of the traitors. We invite you
to choose the right side."

His eyes wandered over the group of prisoners and repeatedly settled on individuals. "Which of you is already Muslim,
or wants to be Muslim?" he asked.

A quiet murmur ran through our rows. The man had not
said what would happen to those who rejected his offer.
Some immediately stepped forward and declared themselves

to be Muslims. They had only been taken by mistake, as their neighbors did not know their true belief. Some also spoke of grudges or slander.

"I have felt connected to your struggle for a long time," one prisoner claimed. "The north of Nigeria must become one hundred percent Muslim again. We must defend ourselves against immigration, and against the increasing influence of the Christians, who want to drive us from our home."

"What is your name?" they asked him.

The man thought for a moment. "Mohammad," he said at last.

"And where do you come from?"

He gave the name of his village: Gavva. It was right next to Ngoshe. Most of the people who lived there were Christians, so I was sure that he was lying. But no one checked whether his information was correct.

"Welcome to our ranks, Mohammad from Gavva," said the chief of the troops who had spoken earlier, and beckoned "Mohammad" to him. Relieved, he switched to the side of the armed men, the "right" side. The men brought him soap and a bucket of water to wash himself, and some clean clothes. "You see? We didn't give you empty promises," the leader said to the other prisoners who had, like me, been watching the scene with keen attention. "Anyone who declares himself a member of the true faith will be welcomed by us as a brother. Everyone else will be our slaves. Because that is how Allah wills it."

Now a whole series of volunteers came forward, declaring themselves willing to acknowledge Boko Haram as the only true Muslims. The men were in a particular hurry. They probably saw it as their only chance of survival, as Boko Haram normally made short work of them. The mere fact that they were still alive was a miracle in itself. I understood their fear. My life is important to me too. Still, it would never have occurred to me to betray my religion. Did my fellow prisoners really think our Lord Jesus Christ would ever forgive them that? Did they think about anything apart from their damned fear, which was driving them into the arms of their murderers?

I watched with quiet horror as more and more Christians stepped to the front and swore their loyalty to the terrorists. They were selling their souls to the devil. I despised them for their godlessness. But secretly I envied them too: how easy it was to take your head out of the noose if you had no scruples.

And again it occurred to me that perhaps it was all just a test. That our God was putting us on trial to find out whose faith was steadfast. I fearfully pressed myself closer and closer to the wall of the building, as if by doing so I could become invisible, or disappear into the masonry. No, I wouldn't waver, I promised myself.

About half of our group converted to Islam—and to Boko Haram. Even two of the women I had come with from Gwoza, and whom I had often seen in church with their families, declared their adherence to the Muslim faith without batting an eyelid. As soon as they had done so they were allowed to wash and given a set of clothing in line with Muslim rules. More and more women disappeared under the black full-body robes that revealed only the eyes. And I didn't really know whether to think they were being particularly clever or particularly stupid. At any rate, they were willingly jumping on the bandwagon.

"You should do it too, you'd be more protected," one of them whispered to me.

"But how can we look our families in the eyes again if we do that?" I whispered.

"Don't think about that. They'll understand."

But I couldn't imagine that with the best will in the world. And I didn't think we would be more protected by Muslim clothing either. Because wasn't it a sign that we were freeing ourselves of our previous ties? Would they really respect us more? Wouldn't it leave us totally unprotected and exposed to the will of an individual?

The fighters greeted the turncoats, but weren't dazzled by their numbers. They deliberately questioned each of us in turn. Each one had to give their name and the place they came from. Apparently they couldn't keep track of which villages they had taken us from.

"What about you?" asked the man who was writing down all our names. He looked a bit older and calmer than the rest of the troop. His clothes were clean and didn't look as if he had spent the past few months as a militiaman in the bush. He also seemed to be of a higher rank than the others. Perhaps he was one of the ones who had been working for the group behind the scenes. In which case, of course, now that they had taken his hometown his time had come.

"Who are you?" he asked.

"My name's Patience," I answered shyly.

"Patience like a hospital patient?" said a second, very young man. He slapped his thigh in great amusement. I think he was trying to flirt with me. "Ha ha, what a funny name."

"No, Patience, like, you know, patience, being patient."

"It's a perfectly ordinary name," said the older man and glared at the younger man. "Where do you come from, Patience?"

"From Ngoshe," I replied. It happened quite automatically. Because Ngoshe was the place my family came from. I still hadn't internalised the fact that since my second marriage I lived in Gwoza.

"From Ngoshe ... you don't say." The older man gave me a penetrating look. He seemed to be thinking. "But aren't you the daughter of Haruna Aiga?"

"Yes, I am," I said, and looked at him in amazement. I was very surprised that the man could mention my father's name so confidently.

"Then you're my niece," he said. And suddenly I knew who I was dealing with. This was my uncle Amadou, my father's oldest brother. Yes, he was a Muslim, I remembered. My grandfather and my grandmother had been Muslims. It was my father and his next-eldest brother, the one who lived next door to us in Ngoshe, who had broken with family tradition and converted to Christianity.

I knew the reason for this from childhood stories. Apparently my neighbor-uncle had once had a car accident in which he had almost lost his life. Even though there was hardly any hope left, the people brought him to the mission hospital in Gwoza. And the Christian doctors there stitched him back together in a miraculous way. My uncle and my father were so impressed by their skill and helpfulness that they had gone on to assume their faith—out of gratitude, to some extent.

As a child I had always taken it for granted that they were both Christians, even though the rest of the family clung to the Muslim faith. After all, there were many mixed-religion families. As I have said before, people often change religion for reasons of career or politics. There's nothing unusual about that. On the other hand, their families were seldom sympathetic. The older relatives often saw it as a scandal when their children left the faith community. Perhaps, it was dawning on me now, that was why we had so little to do with the Muslim side of the family?

The last time I had seen Uncle Amadou had been at my wedding, the first one. On that occasion he had come from Ashigashiya and even brought me a present: a beautiful fabric from which I was to make myself a dress. After that I had never heard anything about him and his family again. What an incredible stroke of luck it was, meeting him again here and now!

"My dear uncle," I said excitedly. "I'm so glad to see you again!" I spontaneously fell in front of his knees. He looked embarrassed.

"Stop that," he whispered. "Stand up."

"Please save me," I pleaded, "tell them not to harm me, my dear uncle."

I didn't know if he was a dear uncle or a wicked one. Only that he was my last remaining hope.

"But child," Uncle Amadou said in a reassuring voice. "No one wants to harm you. We all want the best for you."

He pulled me to my feet. What a curious remark, I thought. What did he mean by "the best for you"?

"Your family has strayed from the right path. But I will make sure that you find your way back to the true faith. I want you to convert to Islam."

"But Uncle Amadou," I said nervously, "you know that we're Christians. I can't just ... "

"Of course you can, and you will," he interrupted. "Forget your past. It doesn't exist anymore: join us and become a warrior's wife."

"How can you say that? You know I'm already married."

"You're a widow," he replied frostily.

I felt great fury welling up in me. So my uncle knew that my first man had died. Did he also know that his friends had murdered him? Had he perhaps even worked closely with them? I wanted to shout at him and tell him they were all murderers. That they had my mother on their consciences. But I bit my tongue. Don't squander your last chance, I warned myself. With great self-control I said, "I'm not a widow any longer. I married again."

"An infidel?"

"A Christian."

"That doesn't count. That doesn't matter anymore. The marriage is hereby annulled."

I glared at him furiously. Had my uncle no sense of honor? Did he want to ruin our family's reputation completely? "Do you want to turn me into an adulterer?"

"Not at all! It's as I say: a Muslim woman cannot be the wife of a Christian."

"But I'm not a Muslim."

"Yes, from now on you are."

I was completely beside myself when he talked to me like that. My own uncle! What had got into him? I felt I was looking at an emotionally frozen stranger.

"Say after me," he ordered. *"La ilaha illAllah Muhammadur*—I declare that there is no god but Allah, and that Muhammad is his messenger."

I held my tongue.

"Say it!" he roared.

Uncle Amadou slapped my face. I began to cry. Two of the men began beating me. They also jabbed me in the side. I was terribly afraid for my baby. Might it be injured by their blows? Or even leave my body? "Yes, I'll say it: *Illalala . . . "*

I deliberately came out with some kind of nonsense, certainly not the Islamic confession of faith. But they didn't notice. Or at least they seemed happy enough.

"You see," said my uncle, "it's fine. And from now on you're not Patience anymore. Your name is Binto."

"Binto?" Had he completely lost his mind?

"Yes, that's your Muslim name. That's the one you answer to."

I stared at my uncle and couldn't work out what on earth he was saying. Did he really mean all that? Was he speaking out of conviction? Or was he afraid that they would kill him if he didn't play according to their rules? For our family this was all a disaster. How would Uncle Amadou ever look my father and my uncle from Ngoshe in the eye again? As I have said, I didn't know him well, but I had the distinct feeling that he wasn't himself at all. Was he on drugs? I tried to study his pupils, but he avoided my gaze.

"Right, let's move on," he said, "I can't waste my time with you forever. Even if you're my niece it doesn't mean you get special treatment."

He told the other men to give me a niqab. "You should be grateful to me," he hissed.

"But Uncle, I'm not Muslim," I said, making one last attempt to bring him to his senses. "And I never will be!"

"No, you are, Binto." He stared at me antagonistically. And I lowered my eyes in shame.

"Kill her if she misses deliberately," Uncle Amadou told his companions. Then he turned to the next prisoner.

# Among butchers

I didn't put on the veil that the men had given me. And I didn't react when they addressed me by the name of Binto. But I wasn't sure whether I was saving my soul by doing so—or consigning it to damnation: wasn't I imposing a death sentence on my child?

The question troubled me a great deal. In the end I wasn't just making decisions on my own behalf: I was deciding for two people, for two souls who were temporarily sharing a body. Yes, it was my body. But I had to treat the situation responsibly, I couldn't afford to be selfish. God had entrusted me with the safety of the little creature that lived inside me. I was carrying a treasure, but a treasure that was also a burden. The fact that no one but me knew this secret, that no one could see my condition, made that burden even heavier.

There was quite an agitated atmosphere in the yard. The new "Muslims" thought they were out of trouble. Some of them even knelt down and started praying in the Islamic fashion. I found their hypocrisy completely repellent. But they were probably driven by the same fear that had made me feel weak and say things that must never reach the vicar's ears.

"Jesus, forgive me," I prayed, ashamed. "I didn't know what else to do."

The wildest rumors were circulating about what the warriors wanted to do with us. Neither the ones who had converted to Islam nor the ones who refused knew what to expect next. "I will never put that thing on," whispered Jara, who had come with me from Gwoza. Like me, Jara, a young mother with a very plump figure, was still wearing the same clothes we had been kidnapped in—a skirt, a tight top and a headscarf tied at the back. In the presence of all those women wrapped in black the outfit suddenly looked like a challenge, if not a provocation.

"Don't you think they'll have more respect for us if we veil ourselves?" I asked her, kneading the veil in my hand.

"I think it's dangerous. They just want us to become Muslims so that they can marry us and we can bring up their children as Muslims too."

"Marry," I repeated. That was just another word for something that must never happen. No, under these circumstances I must never put the veil on. "I'm already married," I confessed to her.

"Me too," she whispered.

"And I'm pregnant," I admitted.

She looked at me in horror. "Don't tell anyone!"

"What are you two whispering about?" said a Boko Haram man. We moved apart. I crept into another corner of the yard. But Jara's words echoed within me. They frightened me, they had sounded so urgent. Obviously she knew something about the way men treated pregnant women. Something that should worry me deeply. That much was clear.

I just sat there like that for a long time. I wondered whether I should ask my uncle or another man for a drink of water. But in the end I decided against it. I didn't want to draw unnecessary attention to myself. The less they noticed me the better.

After a while a truck arrived. It stopped in the street and tried to reverse, flatbed first, into the yard. The Boko Haram people helped the driver maneuver, with wild gestures and noisy instructions.

When half of the vehicle was in the yard, they left it that way. Two of them opened the backboard and ordered all the non-Muslim women to get on board. "Only the young women," they said. "We'll fetch the rest later."

My feelings told me that it would be better not to comply. Jara also looked at me suspiciously. "Where are you taking us?"

"To a safe place," the men said.

"Safe from who? Isn't Ashigashiya safe?"

Instead of replying they struck her with the butt of a rifle and dragged her onto the back of the truck. "We're going to a place where you'll learn not to ask so many questions."

Then all of a sudden my uncle appeared beside me. His eyes were furious, he was clearly seething with rage that

I'd disobeyed his instructions. "You get on there too," he ordered, and grabbed me roughly by the arm. He dragged me to the truck, and I kicked and lashed out. But with the help of a few men who were already waiting on the platform, he pushed me up without any great difficulty. "You wouldn't listen to me," he said, "and now you'll pay the price."

"I'm going to tell my father everything!" I shouted.

But Uncle Amadou was completely unimpressed. "Really?" he said mockingly. "You're hardly going to have much of an opportunity to . . . " And at that moment the driver turned on the ignition, and the rest of his words were drowned out by the loud clatter of the engine.

We drove along the main road from Ashigashiya. Panic broke out on the truck when it became clear to us all that we were being taken away from our home. The women screamed to attract attention. But none of the local people seemed to notice the curious transport being taken from the town. Or at least no one was concerned about it.

No, there was no quick awakening from this nightmare, that much was clear. I was in a world of my own, a world in which I was trapped, and in which only the needs of the terrorists counted. And there was no escape, no way out.

We drove via Pulka toward Bama. Soon we had left the town behind us. The road ran further north through damp, barren territory. To the west lay the Sambisa swamp. After a few miles we turned off in that direction. There was swampy bush on either side of the road. Here no one could hear our cries for help.

The road surface became worse and worse, and muddier. It was starting to rain now too. The lorry jolted through puddles and potholes that opened up in the track. At this time of year it was always a risk taking roads like this, because you never knew if you might suddenly get stuck.

When the pickup slowed down a little, the other women and I began constantly looking for the chance to jump down from the back. But our escorts were careful to make sure that no one escaped from the group.

After about half an hour we reached the little village of Kauri, where we stopped. Even from the back of the truck you could tell that there had been serious fighting in the village: the round huts had been wantonly destroyed, the terrorists had either looted them or set them alight. But where were the people who had lived here?

"Get out," the men commanded. We women exchanged fearful glances. No one moved from the spot.

"What on earth are we supposed to do here?" Jara asked me. I shrugged helplessly.

"Right, now, down you come!" the men repeated, pointing their rifles at us.

So we climbed down from the back of the truck, about a dozen of us. The men below formed a semicircle so that none of us could run away. They waited until we had all climbed down. "Now forward!" they said. "Move!"

We staggered forward, encircled by the men. We actually expected that they would take us to some house or other. But it was soon clear that no one in the village was still alive. Instead the men led us into the fields.

Agriculture in the swamp happens in precisely the opposite sequence to the normal one: it's only at the beginning of the dry season that the farmers sow the seeds that grow and flourish in the damp ground without rain. But now, in the rainy season, the fields were uncultivated and stood partially under water; high grasses and weeds ran riot.

Should I try to run away and hide in the wilderness? I studied the man with the rifle and the machete who was walking along beside me. I had to wait until he wasn't paying attention. But I felt as if I had lead weights tied to my legs.

"Hey, what are you looking at?" he said suddenly. "If you try to run away I'll knock your pretty head off your shoulders."

His words cut me to the quick. It was as if the man had read my mind. I looked away and pretended I hadn't heard. With my eyes fixed straight ahead, I walked on. I didn't once dare to look in the fighter's direction.

After a relatively short march we reached a checkpoint. The fighters greeted their comrades, who were keeping watch. "Who've you got here?" they quipped as they saw us. They looked us up and down and grinned lewdly. "Something for all tastes," one of them said.

They let us pass. Not far from the checkpoint was a little clump of trees; a lot of men were gathered beneath them. They had built a ramshackle camp. I could identify some of them as Boko Haram people at first glance, because they carried guns and machetes. But there were also men who were obviously part of the organization but didn't carry weapons. I guessed that they must be renegades of some kind, or people who had only just joined and who the fighters didn't yet trust.

But above all there were many women in the camp. I saw some in black niqabs, but also others who wore normal clothes and just had a scarf tied around their heads. Most of them were probably prisoners like us. But they were also working. On the very edge of the camp I saw some of them fetching wood. They probably wanted to start a fire. Others were chopping up leaves and tomatoes, probably ingredients for the fighters" dinner. Where on earth had I ended up? Was this place under the open sky one of the notorious camps in which Boko Haram kept the kidnapped women? Were we going to live with them here? Or serve them as slaves?

Our escorts led us quite far inside the camp. Tarpaulins were stretched all over the place to catch the rain. Even so, everything was soft and drenched. The grass was very high and now, toward evening, mosquitoes buzzed around. Insects crawled around on the floor as well. If we stayed here for any length of time we were bound to fall ill.

Some of our fellow prisoners sat on tarpaulins, some on the bare ground. Jara and I were surprised to notice that we knew some of them: they were women and girls from our hometown. Jara discovered some friends from Gwoza who had been abducted at the same time as us. They said that Boko Haram had attacked the town from different sides. And clearly the group had taken many more female prisoners than we had seen in our own neighborhood.

I also met a girl from Ngoshe whom I knew from fetching water in the morning. Hannah had gone to the same well as me and Rifkatu, and we had often exchanged a few words with her there. But since my second marriage I hadn't seen her again. I was shocked by the sight of her: her cheeks were sunken, her eyes dull, her arms and legs scattered with mosquito bites. I barely recognized her.

"Patience!" she greeted me weakly. "What are you doing here? I thought you were in Gwoza."

"Yes, I was," I said. "They attacked us there yesterday."

"They're like wild animals," Hannah said. She told me she had been taken prisoner in Ngoshe on the day of the massacre. The day when so many villagers, including my mother, had been murdered. "I wanted to escape. I ran from the house with my brothers. But they caught us." Her eyes glazed over. "They shot my brothers straightaway."

"What happens here?" I asked her.

"It's hell on earth. They want to turn us into Muslims."

"And if we refuse?"

"There's no point. A human life has no value for them. My advice to you is, don't try to resist them."

There were more things I wanted to ask Hannah. But at that moment one of the men came over. "What do you have to talk about that's so urgent?" he hissed, and held a machete under our noses. Hannah immediately turned away from me. I understood that she was terribly afraid, like all prisoners: Muslims and non-Muslims alike were afraid of the unpredictability of the men with the weapons and their love of violence.

The group that had brought us informed one of the commanders of the camp. He was a tall, slender man from the north. When he saw us, he grinned lewdly, as his guards had done before. But he clearly had more important things on his plate right now than dealing with the new arrivals. "Take them to the others," he said.

So we sat where we were with the girls from our district. They had spread out a few big leaves from the millet stalks on the ground. They didn't have a plastic sheet. But one of the trees sheltered us a little from the frequent showers of rain.

Now, at dusk, they were cooking in the camp. There were several fires. I greedily inhaled the smell that wafted over to us from the cooking pots. It reminded me of one of our Sunday meals. What was it, I tried to remember. Meat? And would we be getting any? As I hadn't eaten for over twenty-four hours I was terribly hungry.

Suddenly I heard the voice of a man raised in a curious kind of singsong. It took me a moment to work out that he was the prayer leader, and that the camp was echoing with Arabic suras. Everyone took the call to prayer very seriously: the fighters immediately dropped everything and assumed the required posture. Only a few of them went on keeping guard. Two fighters hurried over to us and gave everyone who wasn't properly covered up a cloth to wrap around their heads. Then we were supposed to pray—or at least pretend to pray: they forced us to stand straight, raise our hands, place them one over the other on our chests, bend down and put our hands on our knees, and finally throw ourselves down on the ground. And so on.

I joined in as best I could, but it wasn't as simple as that. I had watched Muslims praying quite often. But of course I didn't know the precise sequence. So I just fidgeted around a bit. The other women who hadn't been in the camp for very long did the same: we made a few mistakes that the two fighters who had handed out the headscarves drew attention to by shouting at us or hitting us with the butts of their guns. They also had a whip with them. It hurt terribly when they hit you on the back with it.

I was struck several times during prayer. The girls who had been there for longer were more familiar with the sequence of movements. But I was still unclear what the men were trying to achieve with this action. Did they really think it would turn us into Muslims? Or were they more concerned with the act of subjection? They couldn't seriously assume that we were praying to their god just because they forced us to go through these motions.

I don't need to add that I didn't say the Arabic words, and couldn't even pronounce them. Quite honestly I don't think the men knew them either, even though they considered themselves to be the most pious Muslims of all. They just mumbled some things that sounded a bit Arabic, and we women did that as well. Was their god so superficial that he was contented with this charade? Was that supposed to be a prayer? Silently, secretly, I spoke to my own Lord: "Father, have mercy on us! Don't abandon us!"

Then the prayer was over, and everyone went back to what they had been doing before. The fighters" veiled wives hurried to finish dinner. As I learned, that was their task, since it was important to the men to have their meals prepared by Muslim women. Or perhaps they were concerned that we "infidels" would poison them. I watched as they were served their overflowing plates of food. There was millet porridge and also a rich soup. My mouth watered. The Boko Haram people savored every mouthful. Some of them demanded several extra helpings. Again I wondered if there was going to be any left for us. They couldn't let us starve here!

"You'll taste this dish soon enough," said Jara, who had been watching me. "And once you've eaten it you'll wish it had never happened."

"The smell is making me ill," another woman said.

I didn't understand. Weren't they hungry or thirsty? They gave each other meaningful looks.

When the men had finished dinner, their wives actually called us over to the pots. At last they gave us water to drink. Then they handed each of us a plate and filled it with leftover soup. They were careful not to have too much contact with us, either physically or verbally. Obviously they thought they were superior, now that they were Muslims. In the camp's pecking order they were a cut above the rest of us.

The woman standing next to me took her portion with an expression of disgust. She was the same one who had wrinkled her nose when we had talked about the food: a very thin, but strong- and energetic-looking person who exuded a sense of dignity in spite of our situation. She had probably occupied a superior social situation in a former life.

"I know all these women," she said. "They came to our church every Sunday."

"Where was that?" I asked, as I sat down next to her a little way from the others. I have to admit: I was quietly excited, because at last I was about to have something to eat and the liquid that my body needed so urgently.

"In Kauri," she said. "My husband was the vicar there."

"Kauri," I repeated, and in my mind's eye I saw the ghost village we had wandered through when we arrived. I barely dared to ask, but terrible things must have happened there.

"They killed him in front of my eyes," the woman told me. "They murdered all our men. And these women here," she looked at the fighters' wives with disgust, "want to forget that. They have become accomplices of the people who murdered our husbands, brothers, fathers and sons. They have become involved with the butchers."

"Jesus forgive them."

"No, for them there is no forgiveness," she said. "The burden of sin will crush their souls."

I was horrified to hear the vicar's wife talking like that. Did preachers not always talk about forgiveness and brotherly love, even about loving your enemies? How did that sit with her words? But if I listened to the voice inside me, I could understand her feelings. I too wished the terrorists and everyone close to them nothing but eternal damnation.

"They will roast in hell," the woman said firmly. She had rested her plate on her knees. But she showed no sign of eating any of her food. Even though I was very hungry, that gave me pause.

"Why are you not eating anything?" I asked her.

She looked at me furiously. "Don't you know what's in that soup?"

I looked at my plate and thought, quite honestly, that the mixture of vegetables, millet and meat—yes, really, meat!—looked very enticing. By my lights it was a proper Sunday dinner. "No," I had to admit. "What?"

"That's human flesh," she whispered.

"What??"

"Psst, not so loud," she warned me. "Or do you want to eat me for dinner tomorrow?"

I thought she had gone completely crazy. In camps like this it was easy to lose your mind. But even if her claim was the product of a disturbed mind, I had to admit that it disturbed me too.

I looked round secretly and saw that many of the other women were fiddling rather listlessly with their plates. Particularly the ones who had been longest in the camp—even though they must have been really hungry. When they thought no one was looking, they secretly poured the broth away or picked out the bits of meat to throw them in the grass. They all seemed to agree.

"They don't want to commit a sin," the vicar's wife said. "They know it would part them from their God."

I still wasn't sure whether she was fantasizing or not. Quite honestly I hoped she was. Still, I couldn't choke down a mouthful. When the fighters' wives went round later checking if we had emptied our plates, mine was still half full. "Come on, eat up!" they ordered.

Then I began to retch.

I couldn't sleep all night. I lay among the other girls uneasily, with an extremely queasy feeling in my stomach. Jara slept on my left, Hannah on my right. I could feel their breath. Luckily it had stopped raining. Still, we had to cuddle up together so that the general dampness and the cold of the night didn't get too much for us.

I listened tensely to the noises around the camp, the sounds of animals and people. I was more afraid of the people: every footstep in our direction, every rustle made me start. Because people who ate other people were capable of anything; they had lost their own humanity long ago. In this place I had to be prepared for the worst at all times, I knew that in my belly.

But nothing happened that night. Eventually tiredness took over and I fell into a half-sleep with disturbing dreams: first my dead mother appeared to me, then my father, who had also been murdered in my imagination. Last of all I saw Ishaku with blood all over his face. Those images left me seriously shaken, because I couldn't tell whether my mind was just coming up with evil fantasies, or whether what I saw corresponded to something out there in the real world.

The next morning I felt exhausted when the prayer leader woke us with his singsong chant. First of all we had to join in prayer again. Like everyone else I had slept in my clothes. Of course there was no opportunity to wash in the camp. And no toilet: if you wanted to relieve yourself you had to go behind a tree or do it in front of everybody's curious gaze. Particularly for us women that was a source of shame, as the men didn't look away and made lewd remarks as they watched.

"Come on, show me that fine arse of yours," a man whispered when I actually thought I was unobserved and crouched down behind a bush. "If I like it I might take you." He laughed.

Horrified and confused, I stopped right there and fled back to the group. I soon learned not to get too far away from the others. Otherwise the guards came after us—and you really didn't want to run into them on your own. So I chose to stay near the other women. If you have no other option, you lose your pride.

Sometimes events in this place even made us forget our humanity. We felt like animals.

I discovered that life in the camp was based on a few simple, fundamental rules. They relied on terror, intimidation and constant surveillance on all sides. The different groups held one another in check. The "infidels"—the ones who had originally been Christians and were now supposed to have converted to Islam—occupied the lowest rung in the pecking order. We women and girls were effectively the slaves of the camp and had to do all the lowly jobs: fetching water, collecting wood, keeping the camp clean. We had no rights, and anyone could treat us exactly as they wished.

There were no infidel men among the prisoners: I assumed that most of them had been killed. Only men who immediately joined the group had any chance of survival.

The "Muslims"—those who had been Muslims in their earlier life, or who were considered to be converts and now had to prove themselves as new members of the group—were a rung above us. The women in this category had each been assigned to a different Boko Haram fighter as "wife." They were seldom seen, since according to the strict program of the sect they were entirely devoted to the physical wellbeing of their husbands. In their part of the camp there were a few walls made of plastic sheets to protect them against the eyes of the others when they had to perform their duties.

The Muslim men who already had some fighting experience were our guards; some of them were very young, perhaps even younger than me. They could earn special laurels for themselves if they treated us very severely. Their cruelties were sometimes breathtaking. When they behaved like that they were probably trying to impress the long-serving members of the sect. On the other hand, if they earned a reputation for treating us too carefully, they themselves risked falling into disfavor.

The Boko Haram fighters closely observed the behavior of the newcomers in the group and even kept a record of it. Their regime of terror extended into their own ranks: there was no room for fighters with scruples or any kind of inner inhibitions. Only those who took real pleasure in murdering and torturing "infidels" were considered "true" Muslims, and could go on living among them in the long term. All others ended up on a blacklist. A list that could only mean a death sentence.

So everyone in the camp—from those at the top to those at the very bottom—was acting out of fear, constantly trying to protect their own lives.

As the lowest group in the hierarchy, it was particularly hard for us girls. That began with the distribution of the equipment available in the camp: everyone apart from us had plastic sheets and blankets to protect themselves against the weather. But at night we slept on the bare ground. And if we fell ill there was no medicine for us. And we only had one meal a day: soup.

Of course we lived in constant fear of attack from the men. According to their own rules they didn't have the right to rape us, but in unobserved moments it was bound to happen. No one was repelled if a fighter whose rank was high enough dragged a woman into the field to abuse her. Such behavior went unpunished.

And if they liked us they could force us to become their "wives." Because according to their terms that was our actual purpose. And as they all had several wives, there was a constant need for new candidates. Young and beautiful women, of whom I was unfortunately one, were much in demand. It seemed as if they couldn't get enough of us. Sometimes I even suspected that it was the uncomplicated access to women that drew men to the movement in the first place.

With the so-called marriage—which according to Boko Haram rules could only take place if the woman was considered to be a pious Muslim—one was no longer fair game for everyone, but exposed to the sexual desires of only one man. I saw it as a kind of rapist's charter. Still, some women saw it as a better choice than unprotected status. I found myself wondering desperately how I could avoid becoming an adulteress just because someone had decided I was to be the wife of another man. I always stayed in the background and tried where possible not to attract any attention to myself. Ideally I would have made myself invisible.

The nights were the most dangerous time for us. That was why we always slept in a row, pressed tight against one another. As soon as the sun had set no one dared to move so much as a step away from the others. But the ones on the outside still had visits at night. Unfortunately I know that from my own experience.

The first time I slept in that position, a man suddenly appeared beside me in the middle of the night. I could feel his breath, and his rough hand on my face. He held my mouth closed so that I couldn't scream. Then he dragged me away from the others.

I don't know who he was. I can only remember how he smelled, of male sweat. And that I was terribly afraid of him as he carried me through the darkness.

He leaned me against a tree and rubbed his dirty body against me. His member was hard. Then he lifted my skirt. My whole body was filled with pain when he forced himself into me from behind. He came after a few short, violent thrusts.

After that he simply walked away leaving me in the darkness. I ran back to the others and lay down with them again. No one asked me a single question.

And I felt nothing. I just stared wide-eyed into the dark night.


By day we were assigned to various tasks around the camp: the same things that were considered to be women's work in our villages. With two differences: first of all, we weren't allowed near the cooking pots; and second, we performed our duties under strict surveillance. When we set off to look for firewood, for example, we were always accompanied by one or two more or less low-ranking men. They carried machetes and were responsible for ensuring that we didn't run away. "If one of you tries, she will be killed on the spot," they warned us. And I was quite sure that they wouldn't hesitate to put their threats into action. Anything else would put them in danger themselves.

I could have guessed how great the danger was when I listened to the vicar's wife on that first night. But even though I was frightened by her words they didn't conjure any precise images. I hadn't yet seen the cruelties in the camp with my own eyes.

That would change the first time a Boko Haram fighter became an outcast. It happened out of nowhere, within a matter of minutes.

I don't know exactly how high-ranking the man was—to me he looked like a very ordinary fighter, who hadn't joined the group yesterday. But clearly he had been on the hit list for a long time. It only took a small sign from the commander, that man we had been taken to see on the first day, and a dozen Boko Haram fighters fell on him.

They dragged him to the ground and took his weapons from him, both his gun and his machete. The man apparently knew what he was in for, but he still whined for mercy. "Take pity on me. I'm one of you," he pleaded. "I haven't done anything wrong."

"Shut up," the commander said harshly. "You are a traitor!"

The leader was barely recognizable: his facial expression was like that of a beast of prey. Even though his rage was not directed at me I was terrified of him. A man who looked as brutal as that was capable of anything. "We've been looking very closely at what you do," he told him. "All the men here are witnesses: when we were killing Christians, you deliberately missed."

"No! I swear to almighty God that it isn't so," the man cried, lying on the ground. But the fighters brought their boots down on his back and pressed his face and torso into the ground.

He was a pitiful sight. At first I was surprised that the men could be so brazen as to resolve their internal conflicts in front of their prisoners. But then I realized that the whole thing was entirely deliberate.

"This is what happens to traitors," the commander said in a loud voice, as if he wanted every single prisoner and every single fighter in his troop to watch. They came flowing in to observe the spectacle from every corner of the camp. "All of you, take a good look at how we deal with traitors!"

I sensed that worse was to come. Along with some other girls I stood about ten or fifteen yards away from the man lying on the ground. I would have run away if I could. But I was so frightened of everything that was going on around me that I couldn't bring myself to move from the spot.

I watched as if spellbound as the commander drew his machete from its sheath and raised it into the air. Now it was just above the neck of the man lying on the ground. No! I cried inwardly. You can't do it! Don't do it!

That terrible injustice. The worst thing about it was that you just had to put up with it. I, and all the other figures who had once been human beings, children of God, stood mutely around and watched as another human being was slaughtered. And there was nothing we could do but feel soiled and guilty. But the butchers robbed us of our souls as they made us their accomplices.

The machete came down. It sliced through the muscles at the back of the man's neck and severed his throat. The blood spurted. The head rolled to one side.

*"Allahu Akbar,"* the men cried. They kicked the dead man's head with their boots, and went generally berserk. Apparently with joy because their boss had removed a traitor from their ranks. But perhaps also because they themselves hadn't been the victims. They were in a state of extreme excitement. And the more they feared that they might be the ones lying on the ground next time, the louder they cried: *"Allahu Akbar! Allahu Akbar!"*

As if through a veil I saw some fighters dragging the man's body away. They brought it to the kitchens. Really. Then they stripped it and hacked it into pieces. Meanwhile the fighters' wives in their black veils prepared a fire.

I looked away in horror. Now I had no doubt that the vicar's wife had told the truth.

The women who now belonged to Boko Haram made no secret of what they were serving us that evening. "The blood of traitors makes us even stronger," they said as they filled our plates with soup.

But I couldn't eat a thing. As soon as I even smelled the soup I began to retch, and threw up shortly afterward. Like the other girls, I tried to make most of our macabre meal disappear as furtively as possible. But I had to be careful that they didn't catch me, because I knew what they did to renegades. So I had no false hopes where that was concerned.

That was how things were, evening after evening. Because what I had observed had not been an exception. So-called renegades were slaughtered with horrific regularity in the camp at Kauri. Sometimes they were Boko Haram members who had fallen into disfavor, sometimes they were prisoners or men who had converted to Islam and were accused of betrayal. It always happened in the same way, and was almost like a ritual: the victims were laid in front of the assembled crowd, and then their heads were chopped off. During my time at the camp I witnessed eight such executions. And all the dead were chopped up and cooked, and at least parts of them were eaten in soup.

I very quickly lost a lot of weight, even though I was pregnant. But I preferred to starve rather than eat another human being. I couldn't carry that level of guilt. If I had eaten that meat, it would have poisoned the soul of my unborn child.

On our trips to the river, or to collect firewood, I tried to make up for my lack of food by plucking wild plants and—usually as I passed by—putting them in my mouth. I ate the leaves of the moringa tree and the bright red blossoms of the yakuha tree, from which we usually made tea. Both contain many of the nutrients that my body was crying out for. Sometimes I also picked wild alehu leaves, which taste like spinach and should really be cooked. And if I was very lucky I even found a few okra, which I shared with other hungry girls.

By day, when we wandered around the surrounding area, we were not so closely observed as we were in the camp, even though, of course, we were never unaccompanied. On many occasions I fantasized about running away on one of these outings. But when I told Jara and Hannah what I was considering, they looked at me with such horror that I too lost heart. My friends were right: if we tried to get away and they caught us, they would kill us. There was no doubt about it. Were there no other possibilities?

If we waited until one of the fighters "married" us, our fate would be sealed anyway: my child would be born and grow up as the son or daughter of a murderer. And I would have no chance of a normal life. Even if I managed to escape I would have no future. My family, the people I loved, would inevitably reject me as a Boko Haram wife.

It was an impossible choice. Day and night I racked my brains to think of the best possible course of action. I wasn't afraid of my own death. I was a child of God and Jesus would open the doors to his kingdom to me if I died. I was sure of that. As long as I kept to the straight and narrow, at any rate. So the important thing was to keep sin far away. For that very reason I felt guilty when I considered the possibility of flight. I was also responsible for the child in my belly. Our lives were bound together. And if I destroyed my life, I would destroy my child's life as well. I would become the murderer of the life I carried within me.

The best days for us were the ones when the Boko Haram fighters weren't in the camp. Sometimes during the day they drove around the area. They generally attacked other

Christian villages, robbed them and killed all their male inhabitants. Then at night, intoxicated with the blood of their victims and their own violence, they would come back to the camp. Often they brought booty with them, fresh food, medicine, pots and pans, blankets, tarpaulins to protect them against the rain, kidnapped women.

When the new women joined us in the camp I felt terribly sorry for them. I saw their big, fearful eyes. They were silently asking us, the ones who were already here, what to expect. I wished I could say something to comfort them. But with the best will in the world I couldn't think of anything. Everything that I had had to see here in the past few days—or had it been longer?—showed me that the men who were keeping us prisoner here had lost all human sympathy and any normal human emotions. They behaved like monsters—and they *were* monsters. No, there was no consolation: the women had ended up in a terrible place.

Like us, the newcomers were subjected to careful questioning. The fighters wanted to hear them declare their conversion to Islam, as they had exhorted us to do in Ashigashiya. They pressed their machetes to the new arrivals" necks and forced them to utter the Arabic formulas. Trembling with fear, the women would gabble something incomprehensible that sounded a bit like what they had been told to repeat.

I noticed that one of them had a slightly swollen belly. I secretly observed her. Was she pregnant too? Perhaps because of my own condition I was particularly alert to the possibility. So now I would have a fellow sufferer in the camp.

But clearly I wasn't the only sharp-eyed person there. "Hey, you," I heard one of the fighters say to her. He was staring at her belly just as I had done. "Are you pregnant?"

"No," the woman said spontaneously, "I'm not pregnant." She held her hands over her belly as if to protect herself. It was a helpless gesture, but also one that gave the game away.

"Yes, you are! You're pregnant!" the man insisted. He pulled her hand from her belly. And now everyone else stared at it too. It clearly was a baby-belly. Now that the words had been uttered there was no doubt about it.

"Lie down!" ordered the most senior of the men. He was young, but very brutal looking. Even though he couldn't have been more than twenty he was already missing a few teeth.

The woman resisted. She knew instinctively that she mustn't do it. "Down on the ground, get a move on," he yelled. "We don't bring any Christian babies into the world here."

His inferiors grabbed her by the arms and dragged her to the ground. My heart was pounding as I watched them. This was impossible, I thought, the woman was pregnant! She needed protection! All ethnic groups respected that. But these men ignored that unwritten rule. What were they trying to do to this poor defenseless woman?

After the men had laid her down in the grass, the brutal young man walked over to her. He knelt down and lifted her blouse so that her belly and her breasts were visible. Then he stood up again and drew his machete from its sheath. I wanted to keep my eyes closed, but I couldn't. I watched him running that great knife along her belly as if taking measurements. "All Christian children must die," he said. *"Allahu Akbar!"*

*"Allahu Akbar!"* cried his men.

Then the man slit the woman's belly open. He pulled the unborn child from her innards and threw it into the field behind him.

*"Allahu Akbar!"* the crowd yelled.

They left the woman who would never be a mother bleeding in the grass.

# The demons of memory

Patience has reached an uncomfortable point in her story. I notice that she is losing concentration, and that her descriptions are becoming more and more confused. Often she gazes vaguely into the distance and seems as if she has drifted into another world.

It is the world of horror, which she doesn't really want to think about. She had buried away the terrible things that happened in the Boko Haram camp deep inside her. But now that she is telling me what happened, those events are assuming new life: the demons of the past are coming after her.

"The rest is really unimportant," she sometimes says.

"No, it's all important," I say. "Nothing that they did to you and the other women should be forgotten."

Patience nods. Still, she becomes increasingly tense and laconic. Even the baby in her arms notices that; Gift begins to cough and wail much more often than she did at the start of our interview. She is protesting against the unease that she perceives in her mother.

And her mother understands her protest: she would probably like to wail herself. But instead she regains her composure; she has been taught to keep her feelings to herself. Her crying child also gives her an excuse to interrupt the interview. She walks back and forth with Gift in the yard in front of the church. Patience needs these breaks. It gives her a chance to catch her breath and, for a moment, to escape the acts of cruelty that she is laying out before me.

But her stories are leaving their mark on me as well. Particularly at night, when I lie on the mattress next to Renate, my thoughts are uneasy. Again and again I find myself imagining the scenes that Patience was telling me about only a few hours before. I can't grasp the horror that is still being played out only a few miles away from me. I am especially troubled by her most recent report. Is it really possible that there was cannibalism in the Boko Haram camp? I wonder. Were the members of the sect truly capable of such monstrosity? Or is it Patience's trauma that makes her claim these things? The description of the killings, and of the consumption of human flesh, are a central element of her story. She has mentioned them several times. It seems very important to her that I should know about it.

Because the subject won't leave me in peace, I try to find other eyewitnesses. Several women confirm to me that they saw Boko Haram members drinking the blood of their enemies. I hear several times that they also mutilated the corpses, removing their hearts, for example. But no one apart from

Patience mentions body parts being turned into soup. Among my interviewees, however, she is also the only one who experienced conditions in the Kauri camp in person. And I manage to discover that the vicar's wife she quotes as a witness actually exists: Rebecca finds her name in the parish register of the EYN church. No one knows if she's still alive, or where. So I go on wondering. And once I manage to fall asleep at last, I dream of the horror that Patience has set out before me.

The next day I feel completely exhausted. As always I sit down on the bench under the neem tree and wait for Patience. We have not agreed a precise time for our meetings, I've got used to her just turning up eventually. This morning I wait in vain.

What's up? I wonder. Is Patience ill? I ask Rebecca if she's heard anything about her. She has the number of a deacon who works in the church where Patience is living. But no one answers. I don't know what to do, and spend the day waiting.

When Rebecca manages to get Patience on the phone that afternoon, she tells me that she's been in the hospital with her child. "What's happened?" I ask, shocked.

"She says the coughing got worse during the night," Rebecca translates. "She's been given medicine for Gift."

"And is she getting better?"

"A bit."

"Will she come again tomorrow?"

Rebecca nods. "Yes, if the child is well."

"Get better!" I say.

The next morning Patience again leaves me sitting alone under our tree. Eventually Asabe, our translator, arrives.

Neither of us knows what to do. "She's not going to give up, is she?" I ask Asabe.

"Perhaps she's gone to hospital with the child again."

"Yes, perhaps," I say. But I suspect something else: I think that the interviews have simply got to be too much for Patience. I know that they're hard for her. And that's probably why she's withdrawn.

I've had this experience with several traumatized interviewees before. It was much the same with Farida Khalaf, the member of the Yazidi minority community that was persecuted in Iraq who told me about her time as a prisoner of ISIS: eventually, when the memories become too painful for them the victims of violence find themselves, consciously or unconsciously, unable to continue the conversation. They provoke interruptions, they look for excuses not to go on talking.

Each time that plunges me into a moral dilemma. Of course I would like them to go on telling their stories. But can I force them to do so? "Should we ask Rebecca to phone the deacon again?" Asabe asks me.

"No," I say spontaneously. My experience has shown me that there's no point in contacting Patience by telephone again and trying to persuade her. It would only intensify her resistance. I need to give her time. Then perhaps she'll come round of her own accord.

Only two things help in this situation: a lot of patience, and a lot of empathy on my part.

So I let another day go by, to let Patience recover a little. When she still doesn't show up on the third day, I make a decision: to violent protests from the guard, and without saying anything else to the others, I leave the church compound and trudge off to the place where Patience has always gone in the evening after our conversations. I just need to speak to her in person, to look into her eyes so that she will trust me again.

Patience has told me that she has taken refuge in a little Catholic church nearby. It can't be far away, I think—and ask the first passerby I come across if they know the way. I'm only vaguely aware that I am myself guilty of behavior Renate told me I mustn't engage in. Trust in God seems to be infectious in Africa.

For people in the street I am *the* attraction. A blond European, out and about on her own, isn't something you see around here every day. I get a friendly greeting from everyone. "*Sanu!*—hello, how are you?" they call to me.

"*Lafia*—all fine," I reply, as Renate has taught me. Every traveler to Nigeria needs to know at least those two phrases, she insisted—and as always she was right. People are delighted when I can answer them in their own language.

When I ask them, in English this time, the way to the church, they are overjoyed. I get a thousand different answers—and offers to come with me. It isn't easy to explain to them that I'd rather go on my own. After all, I don't want to be unfriendly.

The church isn't as close as I thought. It's about a mile away from ours, but I have to take several turnings and change my direction slightly. I anxiously wonder how I'm going to find my way back: to my untutored eyes everything looks more or less the same. The roads are unpaved, dusty and scattered with rubbish, with a particularly large number of plastic bags lying around. On either side there are corrugated iron huts, one or two stories high, with their residents sitting outside. Many people have their workshops or little stalls in the street. There are no landmarks that would help you find your bearings.

Still, I eventually reach a metal gate with an inconspicuous sign pointing to the seat of the Catholic community in Maiduguri. Got there!

I knock hesitantly on the door. It is bolted shut. Inside I hear the voices of women whispering.

"Who is it?" one of them calls at last.

"Andrea," I say. "I want to visit Patience!"

I hear the metal bolt being slid aside. Then suddenly Patience is standing in front of me in the doorway. She looks every bit as exhausted as I am. She is visibly surprised to see me just turning up where she lives. "Hello," she says in a friendly voice, and beckons me in.

I step into a yard considerably smaller than that of the EYN church. There is a neem tree in the middle. The church itself is an unadorned building, painted brown and with a corrugated iron roof. Next to it is a shed with mats and woollen blankets on the floor: that is where Patience lives with three other young women and their little children.

The women gather in a circle around me and look at me curiously. They are all wrapped in the traditional bright, printed three-piece costumes consisting of a long, tight skirt, a blouse and a headscarf tied at the back. Patience looks very contented. My visit is an honor to her; proud that I've drawn so much attention to her, she introduces me to her friends. I am painfully aware that Asabe isn't with me to translate this time. But one of the women can at least get by in English, and is immediately given the job of interpreter.

But of course we don't go on with the interview straight-away. We talk about this and that. And the women welcome me with all due honors as a visitor. They bring me a chair, which they set up under a mango tree because it's nice and shady there. I say lots of appreciative things about their court-yard and how pleasant it is. Of course I don't touch the glass of water that they offer me, but they wouldn't expect me to; it's the gesture that counts. Water is always brought for guests as a matter of course.

Then I am invited to visit the inside of the church: a barren hall with neon lights and plastic chairs. Above the altar hangs a giant neon banner, with the words of Psalm 46:10 in big letters and in a slightly altered form: *"Be still and know that I am God. I will be exalted. I will be exalted in the earth (in Maiduguri)."* I praise this highlight to the skies as well, as the laws of hospitality decree.

"How is Gift?" I ask Patience when we are back in the courtyard. "Has she recovered a little?"

"Yes, a bit." She shows me the bag of medicines that she's bought. Apparently she actually has visited a doctor, or at least been to a chemist's shop. "Gift has problems because we lived in a damp shed during the rainy season," she explains.

As if by way of proof the baby coughs. "Will you help me give her some cough medicine?" Patience asks. As I don't have any children myself, I don't know exactly how it works. "You have to hold her nose shut," the child's mother instructs me. I do what she says, somewhat hesitantly. Gift, who is lying on her back, shrieks with fury. Patience takes advantage of the fact to pour some syrup from the bottle straight into her little mouth. Confused, Gift swallows it and then wails even more loudly. But Patience is contented. "That's that done," she says, and rocks the child, who quickly calms down again.

We sit down on the chairs under the mango tree again. At last I summon all my courage and ask Patience why she hasn't come to the EYN church compound over the last few days to continue our interviews. She looks embarrassed, but she still manages to tell me the real reason. "It's hard for me to experience all these things in my mind again," she admits. "That time was so bad . . . " Again that gaze into the void, into the hell within. "I'd really prefer not to think about it any-more." She can't sleep at night, Patience says.

I can understand that very well. I tell her I've felt exactly the same over the last few nights. She is surprised, but com-forted as well. At least she isn't completely alone with the horror in her head.

"It's still important for the world to learn of these things," I say.

"Yes, that's right," she agrees. "Everyone should know what they do with us here—and help us."

She plays with the child, her mind apparently elsewhere. I don't force the subject. At last she gives me the sign that the interview can continue. I take the tape recorder, which I've luckily brought with me, out of my bag and press the start button.

"I'm proud of you," I say to Patience, and I mean it. For her, the eyewitness, it must take a huge amount of courage to describe the barbaric things that she has had to see and experience. And she's agreed to do so. For that decision she deserves the very greatest respect.

Shortly before it gets dark I have to go back: curfew. I feel a little uneasy at the thought of walking back through the twilit streets to the EYN church. "Shall I come with you?" Patience suggests.

"Certainly not." Otherwise she would have to come back in darkness—and risk being ambushed or arrested. "You stay here."

I'll manage, I encourage myself. The girls walk me to the gate. They give me a warm goodbye. "Come back soon!" they say.

Then I step out into the road. Suddenly someone calls my name. Startled, I look into a shadowy face. I recognize the security man from the EYN church, the one who protested so violently earlier on when I left the compound. He followed me secretly and stood guard throughout the whole interview without my knowledge. He gallantly offers to come with me on the way back.

"Thank you," I mumble, ashamed. I am incredibly relieved to have him by my side.

# A friend in hell

The sight of the bleeding woman was too much for me. I stared at her gaping belly and felt my eyes darkening. I probably fainted. At any rate, I can't remember what happened next.

I found myself among the girls again. Jara was fanning me with her bare hand. "It's all over," she said reassuringly, "nothing happened."

Nothing happened? "But the woman ... her child ... "

My former neighbor put her finger to my lips. "Forget her," she said and looked around nervously. "There's nothing we can do for her."

I knew that Jara was telling the truth. As on other occasions when they had forced me to witness their cruelties, there was nothing I could do but stay silent and put up with it. Anything else would have cost me my life. But it's very difficult to accept that. I could do nothing but feel guilty for the death of the woman and her child. I don't know if my friends felt the same way. We didn't talk about it. Each of us tried to digest the monstrosity of what had happened in our own way.

But the event brought me to the edge of my endurance. I was afraid that I would go mad if I saw any more terrible things like that. Or was I mad already? Did this terrible world really correspond to life as I had once known it? Or was I delusional and imagining all of it?

Having been abducted from Gwoza, I had been slung into a world in which nothing was as it should have been. All the fundamental rules that normally apply among people had been abolished and turned into their opposite.

The only friends I had left from my old life were Hannah and Jara, along with a few women I knew from Ngoshe. They were something like an anchor for me, living proof that things had not always been as they were in that terrible camp. That the other, normal world out there had really existed— and probably still existed, unless Boko Haram had destroyed everything.

"Do you think I'm going mad?" I asked Jara.

"No. What makes you think that?"

"Just a feeling. I can't believe that they're really doing these things . . . and I'm watching."

For the first time since I'd been in the camp my eyes filled with tears and I couldn't control myself. Jara touched me gently on the cheek. "We ran into the arms of a group of criminals," she said softly. "But we aren't the crazy ones, they are. May the Lord protect us from them."

"Do you really think he will do that?" I asked her dubiously.

"I'm sure of it."

But I couldn't believe it anymore. I couldn't erase the image of the bleeding woman from my mind's eye. Where, I wondered, had our God been when he should have been protecting her? Would he abandon me too?

"Jara, do you remember what I said to you in Ashigashiya?" I asked her quietly.

She knew exactly what I was talking about. Her eyes wandered to my belly and lingered there. "You mean . . . "

"Yes, exactly," I whispered.

"Don't worry, no one has noticed," she said.

"Yes, I know." But how long would that be the case? My frequent nausea wasn't giving me away, because it was a permanent condition in the camp: many of the women threw up before or after meals. But it was only a matter of time before my condition became visible in another way.

"By then we'll have been out of here for ages," Jara said. But her confidence was false, so I couldn't share it.

"And if not?"

"Then you'll have to marry one of them."

I looked at the ground.

"Patience!" She shook me to wake me up. "You've seen what's happening. Don't leave it too long."


I was at my wits' end. It was clear to me that Jara's cruel advice was correct. In the long term I only had two options: either I became the wife of a fighter, or they would kill me—or rather kill us, me and my child. I couldn't help feeling guilty.

That same afternoon they took Hannah away: even though she was ill, she had caught the eye of one of the fighters. Now he seemed to have been given permission by his superiors to make her his wife. He came with an imam, who quickly rattled through the requisite formulas.

"But I'm not a Muslim!" Hannah protested, when she was instructed to repeat them. They jabbed her in the side with their rifle butts.

"Do you want to be beaten on the first day?" her future husband said menacingly.

Hannah, terrified, shook her head. After she had murmured something they dragged her away from us. From now on she had to live in a plastic tarpaulin shack under a different tree. We never saw her again, since from now on she always wore a niqab like the other Boko Haram women. At night I thought I sometimes heard her crying, but that could have been any of the women.

Wherever I looked all I saw was horror and cruelty: people who forced us to "marry" them, and who chopped each other's heads off or slit women's bellies open. It couldn't be true. Perhaps I had been possessed by a demon, or perhaps I was falling seriously ill.

Jara felt my forehead. "You have a fever, Patience," she said. "Take a rest and get your strength back. I will pray for you."

I had confused dreams that night. Jara kept bringing me water. In the morning I felt a little better, physically at least. Had my prayers been answered? Perhaps we all had to do a lot of praying if we were to get through this misery.

I decided to banish all doubts from my heart, because I needed my God now, I needed him more urgently than anything else in the world. Whenever I had the opportunity over the next little while I talked to him. I knelt down, closed my eyes and started quietly praying. I begged my Lord to lead me out of hell and bring me home. I offered him every imaginable deal. I would put something in the collection next time I went to church. I would start praying three times a day, straightaway. I also asked for the other girls to be saved. "None of us betrayed you. We just pretended to pray to Allah," I assured him on their behalf.

Suddenly I wasn't worried that the Boko Haram fighters or their henchmen, who were always somewhere around, might catch me praying and hold me to account for it. I had no future with them anyway. At best I would become a murderer's wife—and maybe spend the rest of my life with him. That couldn't be the solution for me and my child. The only solution for both of us lay with God. That was why I now dedicated myself one hundred percent to him.

Once a Boko Haram fighter watched me when I was praying. I was terribly startled when I became aware that he was standing next to me. He was a slight, thin man who belonged to the Fulani ethnic group. I was immediately struck by the fact that unlike the other men, who were always creeping around us, he didn't have a leering grin on his lips. He looked rather shy, even though he was clearly one of them, because he wore the Muslim headgear as well as a rifle around his neck.

My first instinct was to run away from him and flee to the shelter of the group. Because, as I have said, it was never a good idea to be alone with one of them. Unobserved, they could do whatever they liked with us.

But something held me back. Perhaps it was his aura. He showed no signs of wanting to come closer, or to go away. He just looked at me. Then he suddenly said quietly in the Fulani language: "You're doing exactly the right thing; do some praying for me too."

I don't know if he expected that I would understand his words. Because we belonged to different tribes, and each of us had a different language, we generally communicated in Hausa. That is the general business language in northern Nigeria, which everyone learns in school. It was the language the Boko Haram members used to talk to us and to each other. So I don't know why it suddenly occurred to this man to talk to me in Fulani. Quite honestly I had the impression that he was talking more to himself than to me.

But I understood him. As Fulani nomads often passed through my hometown, many people in Ngoshe spoke a few phrases of the language. Otherwise it wasn't very common.

"Do you mean that?" I said.

He looked at me in surprise. "You speak my language!" he said.

I think we were each as surprised as the other by our unexpected conversation—and also a little startled. It was the first time a Boko Haram fighter had talked to me like a normal person. Normally they just roared orders at us. It was probably enormously risky for him to talk to me like that, I thought.

"What's your name?" he asked.

"Patience."

"I'm Petrus," he said. It was beyond doubt a Christian name. Had he been a Christian as well? Of course I didn't dare ask him the question. We just looked at each other.

"Praying is the cleverest thing you can do in this place," he said seriously. "Don't give up or you will lose your soul."

I left his words hanging in the air. I should have contradicted a Boko Haram member who said such a thing to me. But I thought I could tell that he wasn't laying a trap for me. I wanted to ask him if he had lost his soul himself.

But before we could exchange another word, more fighters turned up and Petrus turned away from me. He pretended to have been busy with something else. I hurried back to the group of girls.

For safety's sake I didn't tell anyone what had happened to me. I could hardly grasp it myself. Had God sent me this man to show me that I wasn't entirely alone after all?

I couldn't get that curious fighter out of my head. I watched him secretly. I wanted to be quite sure that I hadn't been imagining things.

I noticed that his comrades didn't call him Petrus, but Abu Jihad. That was clearly his fighting name. He was a completely normal member of the group and went off on raids with the rest of them. For a few days I didn't have a chance to talk to him. But then, when we were coming back from fetching water, I suddenly saw him sitting alone under a tree.

I summoned all my courage. "Petrus!" I said to him.

He gave a start. His hand darted to the gun that he always carried with him. When I saw his reaction I gave a start too.

"Sorry," I murmured.

Then he recognized me and smiled at me. "Oh, it's you," he said, again in Fulani. It sounded as if we were old friends. "Did you pray?" What a question! I was really astonished that he was so open with me, even though we didn't even know each other. "I asked you to!"

"Yes, I know. I did," I said, daring to expose myself. It was as clear as day to me that our conversation could be fatal to both of us, if anyone who understood Fulani was anywhere around. "Aren't you scared to talk like that?"

"I am," he admitted. "I don't know anyone here who isn't afraid. But we can't change our fate."

"And what is our fate?"

"I don't know what yours is. But since you pray so hard, I hope that God will hear you soon and bring you back home." He paused and looked thoughtful. "I myself am destined for death."

"What do you mean?" I asked, confused.

"I'm on their list. Don't you see how they cut a different person's head off every day?"

I nodded anxiously.

"It will soon be my turn."

"How do you know?"

"I can feel it. You feel it when your turn approaches. I've only been killing people with half my strength, do you understand that?"

"You didn't want to kill any more Christians."

"In my former life I was a Christian myself, like you," he said. "But then I denied my faith and switched to the wrong side: when I ended up in prison I was worried that they would kill me if I didn't do it. But at least then I would have died with a pure heart. Now I can't make it unhappen."

I looked sadly at Petrus. His confession shocked me—and I didn't know what to say. What I really wanted to do was comfort him. At the same time I knew that he was a murderer. How many lives did this man have on his conscience? Had he killed people I knew?

"If it happens, I would like you to pray for me," he said, "and ask for forgiveness for me. Can you fulfill that last wish for me?"

"Yes," I answered hastily.

"You promise?"

I looked into his eyes, which were kind and sad, not at all like the eyes of a murderer. What did they look like when he killed a person? I couldn't and wouldn't imagine it. "Yes, I promise."

At first I felt uneasy about my promise, but then I made peace with it. Didn't Jesus teach us to forgive? At least Petrus had noticed that he had left the right path, and regretted his deeds. That distinguished him from many other men. I preferred not to judge him.

We became confidants, I would almost say accomplices. Of course, we were always on guard to ensure that the others didn't notice. It was a great help to us that we had a secret language in common. Whenever we had the chance we exchanged thoughts in Fulani. It did me an enormous amount of good to have a friend here.

One morning I was out gathering grass and leaves to lay on our sleeping place, when I met Petrus. He was sitting a little way from the other fighters, fiddling with his gun. I noticed that he was only pretending to concentrate, because he was making the same movement over and over again: putting the magazine in and then taking it out again. In fact he seemed to be thinking about something completely different.

I walked shyly over to him and asked what was wrong. He flinched involuntarily as if I had caught him doing something forbidden.

"You see this magazine?" he asked despondently.

I nodded. "What about it?"

"It's almost empty, they're not giving me any more ammunition."

I didn't know exactly what he meant by that, so I said nothing and waited to hear if he wanted to go on.

"It's my turn tonight," Petrus told me at last. "They are going to kill me today."

"How do you know that?" I asked him, startled.

"They decided yesterday, I heard them talking about it." He was quite sure of it, because he had listened in on a conversation between some other fighters and the commander. "He clearly said my name."

I was deeply shaken. The idea of losing Petrus suddenly seemed unbearable. Apart from Jara, and formerly Hannah, he was the only person in the camp who treated me like a human being. I struggled to think how I could avert this tragedy. But, of course, I couldn't come up with a solution: in the end Petrus was just as much a prisoner as the rest of us. He had to obey the orders of his superiors. We were all trapped.

In the afternoon water supplies ran low in the camp. A group of women were supposed to fill them up again; Petrus was given the job of going with them. He waved to me frantically to come along too. I was busy sweeping the yard. But when I saw him waving at me so urgently I dropped everything and joined his troop.

There were eight young women, and Jara came with us as well. We wandered with our buckets toward the stream, a journey of about two miles. We trudged through the bush and the muddy fields. On the way I didn't exchange a word with Petrus. I just looked at him from the corner of my eye and noticed that he was extremely nervous. He kept pulling at his beard, and his eyes darted in all directions. I wasn't surprised, in his place I would have been nervous as well. Perhaps this was the last walk he would ever go on.

When we got to the stream, he told us to fill our buckets with water. He thoughtfully studied the course of the water. When our buckets were full we lifted them onto our heads, thinking that he would take us back to the camp, where people were bound to be waiting for us.

But Petrus told us to go to the other side of the stream, away from the camp. My pulse quickened when I guessed what his plan was. Had the other girls guessed as well? No one asked any questions. From the corners of my eyes I tried to read their expressions. But they just stared at the path straight ahead, apparently concentrating solely on balancing the water on their heads without stumbling. We stuck rigidly to the path that Petrus had signaled to us. We were completely silent; only the chirping of the crickets sounded impossibly loud while we marched on as if possessed.

We were heading south. Eventually we left the path and continued along a slightly better paved road. A sign told us that it was about six miles to Pulka, the little town at the foot of the Mandara mountain range, which we had passed shortly after we were kidnapped. My heart leapt with joy. That meant we were heading home. By now dusk was falling.

We walked steadily onward. Suddenly, in the twilight on the road in front of us I made out three shadowy figures. They had guns over their shoulders. They were Boko Haram fighters, this was one of their checkpoints. And we were walking straight toward them. Did Petrus not have eyes in his head? If they recognized who he was and saw what he was about to do, they would make mincemeat out of him.

"Petrus," I whispered and tried to tug on his sleeve.

"Stop that!" he hissed.

We were already so close to the men that they could presumably hear us. So I didn't dare say any more. Petrus greeted them. "*Salaam aleikum*, brothers," I heard him say. The other girls and I stared at the ground and said nothing. Some of them pulled their headscarves tighter. Nothing else was expected of us.

"*Salaam aleikum*. Where are you going?" replied their spokesman, a man with a ragged beard and unwashed clothes.

"Our brothers in Pulka are thirsty," Petrus said as if butter wouldn't melt. "We have been told to bring them water."

The fighters looked him and us up and down. But they couldn't see anything unusual about us: to them, one of their men accompanying a group of female slaves was the most natural thing in the world. And the news that we were missing from the Kauri camp clearly hadn't reached them yet. There was also the fact that they were probably all scared to death of making some kind of mistake. Because inadvertently crossing one of their superiors and refusing to obey an order could get them into terrible trouble. In the worst case, it could be fatal.

"Then may Allah go with you," they said politely.

"Thank you, brothers," Petrus replied in a similar tone.

They raised their guns in greeting. Then Petrus ordered us to go on walking. "Come on, you lazy sluts!" he roared. "We want to get there today!"

He didn't need to say it twice: we stumbled hastily on. I prayed to heaven when the men were out of sight.

We walked and walked—but not to Pulka.

# Short-lived happiness

Petrus led us further and further away from the camp. We had now left the paved road. When night fell he told us we could throw our buckets away. "They'll just make it harder for you to walk." We enthusiastically got rid of the vessels. Now the other girls realized that Petrus was serious, and actually wanted to escape with us. We were all delighted. Without our buckets, and with the prospect of freedom, we advanced twice as quickly as before.

We walked all night without a break. I didn't feel tired in the slightest. Of course we gave the town of Pulka, occupied by Boko Haram, a wide berth.

The next morning we reached the long Mandara mountain range, where our home villages were. "You are free now," Petrus told us. "You can go wherever you like."

We could hardly believe our luck. None of us had expected that the nightmare would end so suddenly and so unexpectedly. Weeping, we hugged each other. And everyone hugged Petrus too.

Jara held him tightly. "I will be grateful to you for the rest of my life," she said.

"Me too!" I added.

"I owe you my life. I will always be in your debt," said another girl.

Our savior was visibly overwhelmed. I don't think he knew how to cope with so many declarations of sympathy and gratitude all at once. "You're a good person," I told him.

"Do you really mean that?" He looked at me doubtfully. "What I have done for you can't nearly make up for what we have done to you."

"If you save one human life, you have saved humanity," I replied. It was a Muslim saying. I knew that because our Muslim neighbor in Damaturu had said it occasionally. But I didn't care: the fact that these monsters called themselves Muslims didn't mean that the whole religion was wrong.

"Maybe," Petrus said thoughtfully. "But you'll still have to pray a lot so that God forgives me."

Some of the girls headed off toward their villages. Jara, Petrus and I walked on toward Gwoza. We were already looking forward to being reunited with our families. But we were also a little apprehensive. What had happened at home in our absence? Were all our loved ones well?

As we didn't know exactly what might have happened in the meantime we didn't take the main road to Gwoza but the path over the mountains. It was a very warm, pleasant day. The rain had stopped, at least for now. It was the first time since I was taken prisoner that I had eyes for the beauty of my surroundings. Brightly colored lizards sat on the rocks, darting into their hiding places as soon as we passed. Once we even saw a rock hyrax. And of course baboons and other monkeys patrolling their territory.

We took a rest at a viewpoint high up in the mountain. There was a great view of Gwoza from here, and soon we would be climbing down to the village. I looked into the valley and tried to recognize our compound.

But then I suddenly saw something that didn't fit with the picture I expected. I narrowed my eyes to see more clearly. Was it possible? Smoke was rising from several of the houses. "Do you see that?" I asked my companions.

"Yes, it's smoke," Jara said flatly. "The houses in Gwoza are burning."

We all stared at the clouds of smoke. No one said a word. Instead of the joy I had felt a moment before, the hard fist of fear clenched in my stomach: our escape had brought us straight into Boko Haram's next assault!

Going down into the valley was out of the question now. We stood there mute, looking at the misery being played out at our feet. Luckily we were too high up to make out the details. But having been through such an attack myself, I could imagine the screams of the people being slaughtered or abducted down there only too well. At that moment I hoped only one thing: that my family would not be harmed, particularly my husband.

Meanwhile more and more refugees from the town were streaming up toward us. The whole mountain was slowly filling with them. Perhaps Ishaku was among them. I decided to look for him.

Since I assumed that he would come to our millet field sooner or later, that was the first place I wanted to check. I said goodbye to Jara, who wanted to go to her own family's field. But Petrus, who was from a little village beyond Gwoza, came with me a little way. I honestly had the feeling that he wasn't in a hurry to get home. After everything that had happened he probably wasn't sure whether there was any going back. "I'll go as soon as I know you are safe," he said to me.

I agreed. Together we walked through the mountains toward the field, which was some way below our earlier vantage point. On the way down we met some people from Gwoza. They urgently warned us not to go down into the town. "Boko Haram are setting everything on fire," they told us. "They have come with hundreds of fighters."

I was scared that the people would recognize Petrus as one of them. He was still wearing his gun around his neck. What would people think if they saw us together? And Ishaku? Perhaps it hadn't been such a great idea to let Petrus come with me.

By now we were near the field. I could see the stalks of millet through the bushes. Ishaku would have been working here only a little while ago, and was probably still somewhere nearby. "This is my husband's field," I said to Petrus.

"Then I'd better leave you alone."

I nodded hastily.

"You have been a great help to me, Patience," he said. "I wouldn't have found the strength without you." He took my hand, and I nervously pulled it away.

"I'm sorry," he said.

The man who had saved my life turned round and disappeared.

"Patience!" I heard a man's voice calling across the field a moment later. Ishaku's head appeared among the stalks of millet. "Patience, is that you? Where have you come from?"

I was incredibly relieved to see him, and ran toward him.

"My God, how thin you are! Where were you?"

"I was in . . . in one of those horrible camps," I stammered. But Ishaku wasn't listening. "Was that a man with you?"

"Yes, he brought me here," I answered truthfully.

"Who was it?"

"He was one of them, but he regrets it now. He helped me to escape."

Ishaku muttered something. By now the rest of the family had appeared. The children gathered round me and asked me where I had been for so long. For now I held them tightly in my arms and plunged my nose deep into their wonderful hair. Lara's apparently indifferent expression was like the face she had greeted me with on the first day after I had married her husband. She would clearly have been able to live with it if I hadn't come back. But she welcomed me politely too.

"You must have been through a lot," she said, and gave our husband a meaningful look. "You know what happens in those camps . . . "

Ishaku absorbed the words with a frown. He gave me a penetrating look. "And that man? Why did he help you?" he asked again.

"He just did. Because he wanted to escape as well. He rescued eight women."

"Hm, quite the hero, isn't he?"

"Leave her alone for now," Lara said, interrupting his severe interrogation. "You can see that she's exhausted. Are you hungry?"

I nodded. She gave me water and some of the cold millet broth and the potatoes she had taken with her when they fled. I gulped it all greedily down, and felt as if I had never tasted anything so delicious in my life. Even if their faces were suspicious, I was very glad to be back with them.

We stayed on the mountain that night. It was too dangerous to go back to Gwoza. We spent the night in the cave where the spring bubbled, and where we girls had once fetched water.

The cave was surrounded by undergrowth on all sides. But everyone knew it. So we weren't the only ones who chose it as our quarters for the night. Other Christian families were already camping here. The children thought it was exciting, because there were lots of other children also seeking refuge there. The trip into the mountains was a big adventure as far as they were concerned.

But the adults were very anxious. For fear of being discovered we didn't even dare to light a fire. So there were only a few peanuts for dinner. Admittedly the Boko Haram people hadn't yet appeared on the mountain. But we were sure that

that was what they planned. We knew what their bloodlust made them capable of.

"We can't stay here," an elderly man said as we sat together in the evening. "They want to encircle us on all sides, and smoke us out in the end."

Many of the people sitting around nodded.

"They've already occupied Pulka, Ngoshe and Gavva. Now they're trying to do the same in Gwoza," said another man, probably his son. "By the time I left the town this morning they'd already commandeered all the important buildings."

"The villages on the other side of the mountains are to be converted into camps," Ishaku said.

I immediately thought of my family when I heard that. I quietly asked him if he had been in touch with my father or my uncle, and whether he knew anything about them.

"Your father? No," he said evasively.

"Which family is that?" a woman asked.

I told her the name of our clan. Her face told me that she didn't have good news for me. "There have been some deaths," she said.

"Do you know anything about my father, Haruna Aiga?"

She lowered her eyes. "No, nothing precise."

I didn't have the feeling that I could believe her. Or Ishaku either. Both seemed to know more than they were telling me. But I wasn't sure if I could deal with the truth in my present state, so I didn't probe any further.

Then the men spoke again. "There is only one possibility," said the older man who had been the first to speak. "We need to carry on along the valley to the border." He meant the border with Cameroon, which was about six miles east of the mountain range.

"That's a good idea," his son agreed. "We'll be safe there, and able to wait until the government soldiers have dealt with them. We should set off for Ashigashiya early tomorrow morning."

"But Ashigashiya is occupied too," I cut in. The border town was the first place where I had been held prisoner. The men looked at me in astonishment: a woman speaking out of turn was more or less unheard of.

"How do you know that?" Ishaku asked me.

"Because they took me there."

He didn't ask any further questions. I had a feeling it was embarrassing to him that everyone here knew about my abduction. "Whatever," he said. "Then we'll cross the border somewhere else."

The others agreed, and the matter was decided. We would set off at the crack of dawn tomorrow and try to escape over the eastern side of the mountain.

I spent the night on the bare cave floor beside Ishaku. He had put his arm around me. It felt like a great gift to have him by my side again. As soon as I felt the warmth of his body and heard his even breaths, I felt calm and protected—even though our situation was anything but safe. But right now I could forget all that. For a few hours all that existed was him and me and the little creature that had sprung from our union and now lived in my body.

"I have protected it well," I told him.

"What?"

"Our child."

Ishaku didn't reply. Perhaps he was just too tired.

The next day we were all up bright and early. Some women, including Lara, had made *kunnu* before sunrise. Even if the smoke was risky, they felt that their husbands and children should be given something to eat before their flight. And I tucked in as well, since the opportunity was there.

Then we set off. We fought our way through the undergrowth toward the valley. Ishaku walked a long way ahead of me with the other men. The broken branches cracked when we stood on them, and the moss that grew among the rocks was springy under our feet. I was very cautious: after all I had been through, this last stage of my flight—because that was how I saw it—was nothing. What could happen to me now that God had freed me from hell? At least I wasn't alone anymore, I was with the people I belonged to.

The closer we got to the valley, the more people joined our group; by now I had lost sight of Ishaku and the rest of the family. All the new people had slept somewhere on the mountain and were now, as we were, trying to find a way of escaping. Some of them were able to tell us that Boko Haram had set up checkpoints at this point or that on the road below the mountain, so that we were able to change our route to avoid them. It was a game of chance. According to my calculations we would reach the valley more or less level with Gavva, or a little way south of Ngoshe. There was a lovely farm there with orange trees and a villa where the missionaries had once lived. I only knew it from hearsay. Maybe we would be able to slip through a gap in Boko Haram's defensive wall somewhere around there.

When the red roof of the missionary building appeared among the trees and bushes I suddenly stumbled. It was as if I was being held by an invisible hand. At first I thought I had tripped over a branch or got caught in a vine. I tried to free myself with a few frantic movements.

But I couldn't do it. And then I saw that lots of people around me were having the same problem. I was very frightened. What was it? It was practically invisible. It was only when I looked very carefully that I could see the fine, transparent meshes.

"A net!" a man exclaimed next to me. "Look out! They've put down a net!"

But by then it was too late. With my clumsy attempts to get free I had got myself hopelessly entangled.

I could already hear the wild cheering of the Boko Haram fighters who had been hiding in the bushes and were now running toward us from all directions. Behind me people tried to flee. Ahead of me I saw our men taking out their knives and cutting through the mesh. Some of them managed to escape like that. Others were caught by the fighters.

I was seized with horror once more as I watched them behead their prisoners on the spot with their machetes. They did it in exactly the same way as the men in Kauri, by making their victims kneel on the ground and then slicing through their necks from behind.

After a while several male bodies lay on the ground with their heads beside them. But the fighters were seized with a genuine frenzy of violence. They were even licking the blood off their machetes. And some of them tried to catch it and drink it from the bleeding bodies.

"It's not us killing you: it's God," they cried again and again. They threw the severed heads into the air. "Allah, this is our sacrifice," they bawled, "please accept it from us!"

I couldn't believe what was happening in front of my eyes. These creatures were not human. They had emerged from hell!

No one came to help me. I couldn't see Ishaku or the rest of the family anymore. I assumed that they had reached the valley in a spot where no nets had been stretched on the ground—and it would have been suicide to turn round. Perhaps they hadn't even noticed that I wasn't with them anymore. At any rate, no one came to free me.

# Gavva 1959–2004

The curfew from six makes the evenings very long for Renate and me. Once we've had a picnic snack there isn't much to do in our room in the vicarage.

We spend our time telling each other stories. Having heard so much from Patience, I'm curious about the place where Renate worked as a missionary with her husband around the turn of the millennium. She is happy to answer all my questions.

Renate was based in Gavva. The village is less than two miles from Ngoshe, Patience's home village. Both places are on the side of the mountain away from the A13, in the valley known locally as Bayanduze, "behind the mountain." The name is highly descriptive: until the 1960s, Renate tells me, the tribes there lived more or less in the Stone Age.

On her laptop she has scans of old pictures, very old ones. She shows me the photograph of a laughing woman with a child tied to her back in a leather sling. Her torso is naked. On her upper arms she wears brightly colored bracelets, and chains around her neck. Her chin and earlobes are decorated with wooden spikes. Around her breasts and the child's head the sling is decorated with lots of white cowrie shells sewn into the leather. A sign of wealth: these Pacific shells were used as currency here.

"That was what the people of the Gavva tribe looked like before the missionaries came to the valley," Renate tells me; she inherited the photograph from Werner Schöni, one of her predecessors.

The Swiss founder of the mission station reached the Mandara Mountains—also known in the local tongue as "mountains of the spirit-believers"—in 1959 via Cameroon.

The small tribes who were being hunted and sold as slaves by the emirs had withdrawn to this remote, even hidden region. Unlike the larger and more influential tribes of the Kanuri, the Hausa or the Fulani, they were not Muslim, but followed old African nature religions. The British colonial rulers didn't get involved in the internal affairs of the north. They had made Lagos and the surrounding area their protectorate in 1862, and then declared it to be their Crown colony; the province became the core of the later protectorate of Southern Nigeria. In the south, where there had been missions since the early nineteenth century, the British exercised direct rule. But in the north they only applied the "indirect rule" that was later applied in other parts of Africa as well: they relied on already existing power structures. In concrete terms that meant that the emirs of the north kept their titles and largely operated autonomously within their own realm, although they could be deposed by the British district officers at any time. They collected taxes for the British and issued their directives. In return, the British accepted that sharia would remain the valid legal system, and restricted the activities of Christian missionaries. In this way the traditional structures of domination were preserved for some decades. So, until Nigeria's independence from the British in 1960, the small tribes in the Mandara Mountains were completely untouched by outside influences and attempts at conversion by missionaries. All the tribes there still speak their own language and practice their own version of the old rites.

According to Renate, you can get a vague idea of how these peoples lived before Christianization, and what they believed in, by visiting Sukur, an ancient cultural landscape only about twelve miles southwest of Gavva, on the same long mountain range. In 1999 UNESCO declared it a World Heritage Site.

Their community, like the Guduf tribe, numbers a few thousand people and encompasses several small villages. They are governed from the palace of the chief, the Hidi, which stands on a hill. The fields are arranged in terraces. There are many sacred objects and little shrines that have been cared for by certain families for centuries; they are the spirits of the ancestors, which the people there worship. In certain places on the hills the people also pray to natural gods: Piss, the sun god, Sakur-yum, the rain god, Maila, the god of stars, and Shigal, the guider of worlds. They make sacrifices to them and dance to the rhythm of the drummers for them, just as their forefathers did.

Renate tells me that the people of the Gavva tribe used to live in a similar way.

"Yazhigilmara means 'God' in their language. Bocha is the name of the father of their tribe, the mystical primal ancestor who lives high on the mountain and actually wanted to leave his fortune, the farm and the fields, to his oldest son, Yaghwatada. But through a piece of trickery, his younger brother Gudulf took everything—and from now on Yaghwatada's sons had to live further down the mountain—in Yaghwatatdacha or Gavva, as foreigners call the 'area that runs along the high mountain.'"

Renate speaks the foreign names without hesitation, and it sounds beautiful as she tells me the history of the area. I lean against the wall and close my eyes as I go on listening to her.

"Among the Guduf people, every family had a Tlala, a small shrine in which the ancestors were worshipped in the belief that they had gone down to the Faya: a huge city of the dead in the underworld. In the ancestors' hut the family also kept their treasures, such as spears, bows and arrows, iron points or cowrie shells. Communication with the ancestors represented an important part of the spiritual life. It was the responsibility of the oldest son of a family, and he also had to make sure that the dead were always kept supplied with food in the afterlife. At least once a year they also demanded their festive meal of millet porridge, goat's meat and beer. And woe to them who had only had daughters, who could not assume these duties."

"Could women not perform the rites if there were no male successors?" I ask.

"No," Renate explains. "A man without male heirs would inevitably fall into oblivion after his death. And everything he had built up in his life would decay."

What a long history contempt for women has, I think sadly as Renate goes on with her story.

"Missionary Schöni, who lived for a time with the Guduf people in the mountains, studied all these practices and also learned the language of the tribe. Then he asked their chief for permission to settle in the valley. The chief declared his agreement, but assigned him a piece of land on which the tribes usually fought their feuds: a blood-drenched piece of ground. According to the old beliefs, the spirits of the dead got up to mischief there, and no local person had ever built on that land. That the Swiss missionary built his house there anyway, and seemed to be immune to the spirits, made a great impression on many of the tribespeople," Renate explains to me.

"And it doubtless made them curious about his religion as well: his god, who must clearly be very powerful," I agree, and can't help admiring the missionary for his strategy.

"Yes, Schöni achieved a lot: he and his helpers didn't just convince the mountain people of the power of Jesus Christ, but also persuaded them to give up their old life in the mountains. Up there the traditional believers were chiefly afraid of the Muslim tribes. On the other hand, down in the valley the earth was much more fertile. So moving meant better harvests and a more comfortable life—but also less protection against attacks from other tribes, which had previously made people hesitant about taking that step.

"But the Europeans had an answer to that: the same Lord Jesus, to whom the mountain people now prayed, would protect them in future, they promised. It sounded almost too good to be true. But either way, it did seem to benefit the mountain-dwellers.

"So the people of the Guduf tribe moved to the valley, they took Bible classes and built a church on the instructions of the missionaries. Soon they also followed their advice to put on clothes. Their private parts had to be covered, after all.

"Look at this." Renate flips her laptop open again and shows me more photographs. I see the first eight members of the Guduf tribe to be baptised standing in a tub of water in front of the mission station. They are all young men, including the son of the woman with the sling decorated with cowrie shells. The congregation stands around watching what is happening: about half of them are bare-chested or have their legs uncovered, while the other half are already dressed "decently." Schöni himself wears short trousers. Apparently the influence was reciprocal, Renate giggles: "It happens to the best of us."

By the time she herself came to Gavva in 1999, most of the inhabitants had converted to Christianity long before. Renate still clearly remembers driving into the village for the first time, along a sandy track, and all the little houses and the people cooking and eating outside them, among chickens, goats and sheep. "I felt as if I was driving right through their sitting room," she tells me.

In the forty years since Schöni's first contact with the Guduf a lot of things had happened. The life of the tribe had changed completely. The valley, which people had previously avoided, was now densely populated. The missionaries had helped them to plant orange trees and set up irrigation systems. They had also founded a medical station. Development money from Switzerland, which had been particularly abundant in the early years, allowed the area around the mission station to prosper.

But Renate was especially impressed by the spirituality of the young congregation. "The people of Gavva had adopted the new religion with a great deal of idealism," she tells me. "I have never met such enthusiastic Christians as I have here." After the harvest thanksgiving that I witnessed, it isn't hard for me to believe that.

By way of welcome the village community performed an old rain-making song, in which the men danced stamping around in a circle. It worked promptly. "The rain came only half an hour after the men had finished their dance," she tells me, not without a certain respect.

"Were they Christians?"

"Yes, of course. That's not a contradiction in Africa."

Unlike her predecessors, Renate didn't do classical Christian missionary work. She didn't need to, because it happened of its own accord—via the church itself: any congregation that wanted to be accepted by the synod needed to show at least one hundred baptised members, who give a tenth of their income to the running of the church. Apart from the construction of a church building and the appointment of a vicar, their duties included setting up preaching stations in at least three other places where there were not yet any

Christians, and doing missionary work there. In this way the influence of the EYN church was able to expand—without the addition of Western missionaries—further and further around the region.

So Renate focused on continuing the development work. She was chiefly concerned with the education of women, among whom the illiteracy rate is particularly high: ninety percent of the women in the villages can neither read nor write. "I thought it was important to put them in a position whereby they could at least read the passages from the Bible unaided."

To bring education to small communities and remote villages, she invited a deputy to come to Gavva: he or she would be given a two-week crash course as a teacher. Then they were sent back and the education began. It could only happen during the rainy season, when the women didn't have to work in the fields. For the first two years reading and writing were on the timetable, and maths and religious studies would follow later. But for many women who hadn't gone to school as children, even learning the letters was a real challenge.

"They had problems recognizing geometrical figures," Renate recalls, "such as the difference between a rectangle and a circle." So the teachers spent days drawing circles in the sand—the letter "O." Recognizing the length of lines, one of the key qualifications required for reading, was equally alien to the women. They practiced by collecting sticks of different lengths. "If you have worked all your life in the field, your eye must get used to these things."

In the five years that she spent in Gavva, Renate founded around a hundred little schools in the nearby and more remote villages—work that she remains proud of. The progress and improvement in living conditions were quite tangibly apparent to her. "You can do so much with so little; Gavva was in a very good way at the time," she says. Her voice sounds melancholy. "It was a wonderful patch of ground. I felt great there—and also safe."

She tells me about the mission house and her garden with the old orange trees and all the flowers that grew there. Particularly in the evening, when it became a little cooler, their blossoms had the most wonderful fragrance. "The old people warned us: they knew that this place was a battlefield." She reflects. "But I couldn't have imagined such a positive development turning into its opposite . . . "

I feel a horrible suspicion creeping over me when I hear her talking like that. I almost hesitate to express it, but then I summon the courage. "If you hadn't converted the people to Christianity, they mightn't have so many problems now," I dare to say at last.

Renate looks at me despondently. "What makes you think that?"

"Well, because then they would still be up in the mountains—and Boko Haram would probably have left them in peace."

"I hardly believe that," she says. "Boko Haram don't just kill Christians, they kill people of all other faiths." She explains to me that the radical Islamists hate the worshippers of the natural religions even more than members of the so-called religions of the book, which according to the Qur'an include not only Muslims but also Christians and Jews. "Just look at what happened to the people of Sukur. Did staying in their mountains do them any good? No!"

"What did they do to them?" I ask nervously.

"They shot them down and destroyed their sacred objects—just as they did in Gavva, Ngoshe and Gwoza. Hundreds of men were killed, and a third of their people are supposed to have been abducted."

I am very quiet, I didn't know that. "I wasn't trying to say you missionaries are to blame," I say in a small voice. It sounds like an excuse.

"And we aren't. If a group of murderers decides to commit a crime, no one but those murderers is to blame."

"No, of course not," I agree straightaway.

"No one could have predicted that," Renate goes on. "Even my husband and I didn't notice what was brewing."

At that time violent conflicts between Christians and Muslims were only taking place in Jos, a town right on the unofficial border between the Muslim north and the Christian south. A lot of churches are based there—and the very Christian lobby annoyed the radical Islamists. Armed clashes often broke out there.

But in the province it had always been peaceful in her day, Renate assures me. Apart from a few petty jealousies there had been hardly any animosities between Christian and Muslim inhabitants. "It just wasn't an issue between people. One was Christian, another Muslim—end of story. At Christmas and at the end of Ramadan they wished each other a happy festival."

# Gavva 2015

"That'll teach you to accept the white man's religion," said the men as they drove us towards Gavva. They had only killed the men. They took the women and children prisoner. "So where's your white god now?" they asked. "Why isn't he protecting you?"

I was in a state of both shock and despair. It couldn't be, I kept thinking: after only one day of freedom, here I was in captivity again. Could the world really be so horrible? There must have been a terrible mistake.

"My God, why are you doing this to me?" I whispered— and was startled to realize that I was asking almost the same question as the men. Was I allowed to reproach him? I couldn't help it. After believing that I'd survived everything, I was bitterly disappointed.

As I already had some experience of captivity and knew what to expect from my tormentors, I desperately looked for a chance to escape the column. But the men, probably about two dozen of them, surrounded us on all sides. "If any of you try to escape, the same thing will happen to you as happened to the men," they threatened.

One did try. She was a young woman who had sat in the cave with us in the evening. She pulled away from her guards and ran into the thicket. But she only got a few yards. One of the men shot her from behind. He hammered a great salvo of bullets into her back from his machine gun. She collapsed and lay motionless on the ground. They left her body there. "The vultures can have her," they sneered. "Any more of you fancy a try?"

They brought us to Gavva. The town consists of three settlements, Gavva-I, Gavva-II and Gavva-III, which run along the slope. Members of the Guduf tribe live in all three settlements; the members of the group used to live further up the mountain.

The former mission station was in Gavva-II, and thus in between the two other settlements. There were also several churches here, two schools and even a Christian cemetery. Much of this had been built by the whites, who had worked here until a few years ago. They had ensured that the place was in a reasonably good economic state, which was why all the other villages had been a little envious of Gavva, including the people in my home town of Ngoshe.

When our march took us past the property of the missionaries, I cast a curious eye over the garden, which lay behind a big iron gate that bore the inscription EYN LITERACY PROGRAMME. No one had so far taken the trouble to remove the sign. The garden was almost a forest, there were so many tall trees. Bright, ripe oranges hung from some of the trees, and Boko Haram fighters were camped among them. Right at the back, at the end of the drive, I could see the missionary house. The old villa shimmered white in the middle of a sea of magenta bougainvillea blossoms. Only at second glance did I see the traces of soot on the façade. There had clearly been attempts to destroy the building before the commanders decided to use it as a place to live. The old swimming pool was no longer filled with water, but was being used as a rubbish dump.

The whole place was a curious mix of past and present; in the interplay between the two the leftovers from better times and the raw violence of war looked rather strange. For me the occupied missionary estate was a symbol of the decline of a flourishing town. Nothing would remain of the former glory and affluence of Gavva after the arrival of this gang, I knew. It made me sad to see it.

We passed the cemetery. Again I caught my breath. The holy warriors had raged here too, and in a way that is incomprehensible in our culture. All the crosses had been taken down, the graves desecrated, leaving only gaping holes. The bones of the dead lay scattered everywhere.

What an incredible act of blasphemy! I shuddered at the sight of it. How could they dare to disturb the rest of the dead? Weren't they afraid of the consequences? After all, everyone knew that the spirits of the ancestors could become very angry. Would they now haunt the place? Would their rage be directed at the living?

I felt very sorry for the people of Gavva, for what had been done to them. I hoped their ancestors understood that there was nothing they could do. Because the desecration of those graves was not their doing. Certainly their descendants had the duty to protect and honor the resting places of their ancestors. But what were you to do if a horde of murderers attacked the village? Nothing at all? You were simply at their mercy! I hoped that the villagers wouldn't be exposed to the anger of the ancestors forever.

The other prisoners were open-mouthed as well. They turned away in horror when they understood the monstrosity of the deed. I think the Boko Haram fighters brought us here deliberately: they wanted us to see their crimes. They were showing us that they had no scruples or respect for our Christian faith, or indeed our traditional beliefs, that they did not fear our God. Because would he not have held them to account long ago if he was really so powerful? In their eyes the desecrated graves were the best proof that he didn't exist.

"Lord, let them regret this crime," I whispered.

Then they led us further toward Gavva, which was once, as I have said, a well-presented village. Here too some of the people still lived in the traditional round mud huts. But some had rectangular houses made of stone with corrugated iron roofs that kept the rain off. Some huts even had electricity and running water.

Normally there are lots of things going on in our streets. Children flit back and forth between the farms, street-sellers praise their wares and the women of the village chat as they shop, while the old people sit outside their huts and observe what is going on. But today it was deadly silent. There was no one about. In many places the settlement looked properly orphaned. In others, it seemed we could hear voices behind the walls—as if there were still people there. That struck me as strange. Had some families barricaded themselves inside their farms? Or did the fighters live there? At first I didn't understand how Boko Haram had reorganized life in Gavva.

They brought us to a walled compound. A man guarded its entrance. When he saw us coming, he greeted the other fighters and let us through.

We stepped into the spacious courtyard, which contained several round huts. The large enclosure must once have belonged to a rich or at least a large family. But now the whole courtyard was full of women, all veiled in the Islamic style, showing as little skin as possible. They were of every age: elderly, young, a lot of children. But only girls.

"This is your new home," they said to us. "You will live here until we have turned you into respectable Muslim women."

"What do you get out of this?" one of them asked.

"You'll find out sooner or later," a man replied.

"Once we've converted you, we'll distribute you among the fighters," another blurted out.

Some women protested loudly and pointed out that they were already married. But I said nothing. I knew that didn't matter to them. "Your husbands are dead," they said. "Didn't you see us cut their throats? So be glad if you end up with one of us."

They began by weeding out the boys from the group. "You come with us," they said to them. "Or do you want to stay with the women?"

The boys looked nervously at their mothers. Some of them shook their heads, others went to the men of their own free will because they thought it was an accolade of some kind.

"You're not taking my child," one woman called, and held back her son, a boy of about eight, when he was about to march off.

"Oh yes, we are," the men said and pulled him away from her. The boy looked rather confused. "After all, he isn't a girl."

Another woman who had an even smaller boy with her struggled to hide him under her skirt. We stood in front of her so that the men wouldn't notice. But the child was too curious, and peered out from under her clothes.

"Come out of there," a man said when he saw him. The frightened boy obeyed. His mother began to cry.

"But he's only five years old," she said, "he's far too little to be without me!"

"Nonsense, he is the perfect age," snapped the Boko Haram people. "We will make a real man and a warrior out of him."

No amount of protest by the women helped: they took their sons away. The boys who didn't go of their own accord were violently dragged from their mothers. They even pulled male babies out of their mothers' arms. But they killed the babies with machetes, right there in front of us. I don't know what their plans were for the older boys. Perhaps they wanted to train them to be fighters. But only we women and girls were left behind in the compound, the mothers among us almost insane with grief, the rest of us frozen with shock.

I was in total despair. After the men had left us alone, I crouched down in my corner and wept. I simply couldn't grasp what a mean trick fate had played with me again in the past few hours. What had gone so terribly wrong that I found myself in such a terrible position?

I felt as if I had been through all this before. Essentially what was happening here in Gavva was like what I had already experienced in the Kauri camp.

The hell that I had so recently escaped had very quickly caught up with me again. At the beginning of my time in Gavva I simply couldn't accept it. I crept away inside myself and acted as if the outside world didn't even exist. Perhaps these figures were only products of my imagination, or perhaps I'd been put under a spell. Was that why my family had left me behind?

I sat there in silence and watched what was going on around me. Life in the Gavva camp—because these three settlements could hardly be described as a village—was more strictly organized than our everyday life in Kauri, which had looked different every day. Our daily jobs and tasks had varied greatly according to the raids undertaken by the fighters, the mood of the commander and the weather.

In Gavva it was quite different. There was a very strictly regulated timetable: at five in the morning the fighters woke us with the call of the muezzin, and we had to go to first prayer. Then we had our morning wash. The fact that only women lived in the huts in our unit made that a great deal easier: at least we were able to perform our bodily functions in private.

At daybreak we went to the primary school along with a group of guards, some of them boys. The school was at the other end of the elongated village. It took almost an hour to get there. We marched past fields and farms, which were either empty or occupied by Boko Haram people and their wives. According to the women all the Muslims in the village had joined the movement, which also meant that they were able to keep their property.

Once, when we were crossing the fields, I saw a group of men engaged in weeding—all of them gaunt and tattered figures. Who on earth were they, I wondered. At any rate they weren't fighters or members of the organization. And then I noticed that some of the women around me were glancing around at them. "Yousef!" one woman suddenly cried and waved like mad until one of the guards struck her with his gun. Then I understood: these men were the Christian former inhabitants of Gavva. I later discovered that they were kept prisoner in a school in another part of the village.

I was honestly surprised to see that they were alive. Normally the fighters made short work of men of other faiths. But apparently they were able to use these men as slaves for the harvest. The fact that they were allowed to work on the farm was very different from the way things had been before: it might have represented an attempt by the group to become settled and no longer to live on plundering raids. Were there sometimes simply not enough Christian villages for the fighters to loot, because their own empire had become too big?

Increasingly I had the impression that Boko Haram had turned my home into an enormous prison camp. The boys were being trained as fighters, the men were slaves in the field, and we women and children ... well ... they probably expected us to be sexually available for them. And in the meantime they were trying to convert us to Islam, to make us into compliant wives for them. What madness!

I also thought of my family. Were my father, my uncle and my brothers in Ngoshe now living out their lives as slave laborers, as these men were doing? Were they still alive at all? And Ishaku? What had happened to my husband? Had he and Lara made it to Cameroon, or had they also been taken prisoner? Perhaps, I dreamed, I would one day find myself in the same position as the woman who had happened to see her husband in the field.

Then we reached the school, a plain stone building with two classrooms. On the white outside wall the fighters had painted Arabic characters, which I couldn't read, even though I had learned them in school, because that's how Hausa is written. As I approached them I couldn't help but shudder: the letters were made of dried blood. "It is the blood of a *takfir*, an infidel," they told us. "He deserved only death. God himself killed him through our hand."

"Yes, God gave us this task," agreed their imam, who had a long beard and a turban, which made him look like a real Arabic scholar. "He demands that we make you all into Muslims. Those who do not become good Muslims must die."

In broad brushstrokes he had been outlining the program for the education that was to come: it was designed to familiarize us with their religion, as part of the conversion process.

Generally the imam first read to us from the Qur'an, in the Arabic language. Half asleep, we listened to the incomprehensible singsong. Then he gave us a summary of what he had said to us. And after that we spent a lot of time repeating individual sentences as a chorus. His goal was to make us learn as much of the text by heart as possible.

This man was a genuine fanatic. He endlessly ran through the suras with us. He seemed completely obsessed with his mission to persuade us of the foundations of his faith. If one of us made a mistake she immediately received a sharp rap with a stick on her knuckles or her back—particularly toward the end of the lesson, when our attention wandered because of the heat. Quite honestly we weren't very surprised by this, because even at normal state schools in Nigeria being beaten is part of the education process.

Through the interpretations of the text that he gave us, I learned a lot about the worldview of Boko Haram. "Muhammad was a very wise man," he said, for example. "But he was not just a preacher. He created a perfect state according to the law of God. Under his rule there was no criminality and no injustice. Because he ensured that everyone stuck closely to the rules. Adulterers were stoned, thieves had their hands chopped off."

Then he looked around to check that we were all paying attention. If he had a feeling that one of the women was daydreaming, he asked her, "What happens to thieves?"

"They have their hands chopped off," she would answer if she didn't want to be beaten.

"Exactly. And that is the ideal that we ourselves pursue," he continued immediately. "We will tolerate no one who disregards the laws of God. What do we do with the enemies of God, the unbelievers and those who fall from the faith and turn against us?"

"We cut their throat," we answered in chorus. "We must finish God's work. So he commands it."

We spent the whole day on lessons of that kind. At midday we took a break, but then it continued, again for several hours. It was only in the late afternoon that we were escorted back to our prison by our guards.

Several times I saw women trying to escape on these walks. But they were quickly captured and beaten, and sometimes they fired at them. At first I was shocked by the cruelty with which they punished all escape attempts, again and again. But eventually I almost got used to it. The continual sight of violence left me desensitized: I didn't expect anything else.

When we returned to our quarters at last we were very tired. We didn't have to fetch our water in Gavva, because the men wanted to stop us walking about in the street. The boys fetched the water for us. But we cooked the food that they provided for us. Usually they gave us some millet, sometimes some okra or potatoes. It was never enough for more than one meal a day. Still, I was glad that they let us prepare our own meals here. I can't say if they held the same funeral parties that I had observed in the Kauri camp. As we lived separately from the men, I found out less about their rituals.

But our evenings in Gavva were still not free of anxiety, let alone relaxed. Quite the contrary: it was at that time of day that the fighters turned up looking for women to marry.

I still remember the first time: at dusk, when we were all gathered in the courtyard, three men suddenly came to our compound. One of them was very young, perhaps seventeen or eighteen. The others looked older, perhaps in their mid-twenties. They were wearing typical dress: a head-covering and a Salafist beard. One of the two older ones was even wearing a turban, and his beard was a bit longer than most, which made me conclude that he was one of their preachers. And of course they were all armed with guns or machetes.

The women cowered in a corner when they saw the men coming through the gate. The ones who had been here longer than I had knew exactly what would happen next. And it wasn't good.

"On your feet!" the men ordered. "We want to take a close look at you." They made no secret of their plans. I tried not to enter their field of vision and went and stood inconspicuously at the side. Some of the younger girls hid in the same way. But they were the ones the men were interested in. "Hey, don't do that," they shouted. "Come forward!"

They dragged a girl of about twelve out from behind her mother. The girl was shaking from head to foot. "You're the one I want," the eighteen-year-old announced, "you are to be my wife."

The young girl didn't say anything and stared at the ground. But her mother could control herself no longer. "You should be ashamed!" she shouted at the young man. "She's not even a woman yet and you know that! But you've had your eye on her before, haven't you? You were creeping around our house all last year."

"Shut up!" he roared and struck her in the face. So the two of them knew each other from their former life; perhaps the boy had been a ne'er-do-well from the neighborhood who had been after the girl. At least he was probably one of the former Muslim inhabitants of Gavva who had joined Boko Haram and declared their deeds to be *aikin Allah*, the work of Allah.

"According to the Qur'an she's old enough," the imam said. "Nine-year-olds can get married. It is written."

The other, slightly older man also chose a girl who was exactly as young as the first one. They clearly liked it when they'd only just reached sexual maturity. But with these two I wasn't at all sure because they had no breasts, and their features were those of children.

They were both in a state of complete shock. They wept and asked the men to spare them.

"Shut up!" the imam ordered. "Say after me: *Bismillah al-Rahman ar-Raheem Al hamdu lillaahi rabbil 'alameen* ... In the name of Allah, the merciful and compassionate, praise be to Allah, the Lord of the world ... "

I recognized *al-Fatiha*, the opening sura of the Qur'an, because we had been through it with the imam in one of our first classes. It's very important to Muslims, and a crucial part of many of their prayers. So it is indispensable at weddings. The loud declamation of the sura is seen as a blessing for the union. But the girls kept their lips tight shut and didn't say a word.

"Would you get a move on?" the imam said menacingly. "If you don't want to get married we'll take you to the Sambisa Forest, where the mosquitoes will devour you and you will get nothing to eat. So, are you going to be good wives, or will we have to force you?"

When the girls still said nothing, the cleric gave the men a sign. They grabbed their chosen girls and beat them. They gave them a good thrashing. They didn't stop until the two girls started whimpering and asking for mercy.

Then the imam asked them again: "Will you say the *al-Fatiha* now?" Again he began to recite the Arabic words. Afraid of being beaten again the girls didn't dare to resist any further, and murmured something. No one really cared if it was the words of the sura. The mother of the first girl sobbed so loudly that no one could make out a word. But the main thing was that the illusion of Islam was preserved.

To maintain the appearance of a legitimate wedding, the men then ostentatiously counted out a "bride price" of 500 nairas to the girls' families. About twelve dollars. And that meant they were married.

"Swine," hissed the mother of the first girl when the eighteen-year-old handed her the money. She spat in front of him but hid the banknotes before he could take them away again.

The second girl had no family members in our unit. She was allowed to keep her bride price herself. So everything was in order, at least from the imam's point of view.

The men dragged their new "brides" outside like booty.

It was like that almost every evening. Men came to view the brides. Soon they had "married away" all the young girls of the age they found attractive. We knew they lived with them in the houses and farms that had once belonged to the Christians, not very far away.

For those of us who were living in the unit, the disappearance of the girls meant that the warriors would now seek out older women, or go after the children. Usually they chose the latter. That was always horrific for the mothers and daughters. There were many discussions about the age of the girls. The mothers always claimed their daughters were younger than nine, the magic threshold. The men disputed it and accused them of lying. They demanded that the imam perform the wedding ceremony anyway, and that was usually what happened. It was only when they discovered that the bodies of their "brides" were actually too small to have sex with them that they brought them back and chose another one instead.

The more our ranks thinned out, the more nervous I became. Unlike in the Kauri camp, there were no additional women joining us, because the fighters went on fewer raids. That made my own situation dangerous. Admittedly, at the age of eighteen I wasn't one of the very young women they immediately chose, but I wasn't one of the old ones either. So I knew that it was only a matter of time until one of them went for me.

One evening—I think I'd been in Gavva for three weeks— another marriage delegation came to our compound. I was poking the fire, and interrupted what I was doing when I saw them coming. There were six of them. I knew one of the fighters, because he was one of our guards. He was a strong man in his mid-twenties. He had often given me lustful looks. So I flinched when he came purposefully toward me. I immediately looked away. Maybe he hadn't been looking at me?

"Hey, you!" I heard him say. My heart thumped with fear. But I didn't react. I stared stubbornly at the firewood.

"Hey—what's her name?" he asked the others.

"Her name is Patience." The name Binto, which I had been given in Ashigashiya, had only applied in Kauri. No one here knew it.

"Hey, Patience!" he repeated. I still didn't look at him. Now he was coming too close to me.

"My name is Mohammadu," he said quietly. "I've been watching you for a while. Would you like to be my wife?"

I shook my head violently.

"You know I can force you," he said.

"You would be sinning. You mustn't take another man's wife," I said. "I'm married already."

"But your husband is dead!"

"I don't know that. And because I don't know, I can't marry you. Please understand that."

He said nothing at all for a while. I expected him to draw his machete at any moment and press it to my neck to force his will upon me. But he did nothing of the sort. He didn't shout at me or hit me. "Fine," he said. "I won't take you by force, because I really love you. But please at least think about my offer. It could be good for you."

His words made me think. I watched after the group for a long time as they left. All the men apart from Mohammadu had chosen a wife and "married." But he kept his word and didn't force me. Even though the others looked at him slightly askance, he went home alone. I thought well of him for that.

But would he leave me in peace in the future? Or did he think I might change my mind once I'd had some time to think? And how would he react if I didn't? How tolerant was he?

I didn't see him over the next few days. Quite honestly I was glad of that. I thought long and hard about whether marriage might be a possibility for me. Because by now I had a very different and far bigger problem. When I looked down at myself I could clearly see my clothes stretching across my belly. My pregnancy was slowly becoming visible. That frightened me. Only recently I had seen them kicking a pregnant woman in the belly until she curled up with pain and at last had a miscarriage. They would treat me like that, or worse. Dear God! I thought: I didn't want that to happen to my child. I had to act before it was too late. I hoped nobody else would see the change in me.

I listened to my inner voice. Could I palm off someone else's child on Mohammadu? If I could have saved it like that, presumably I would have done, I think in retrospect. But at the time I didn't see that possibility.

What I saw, on the other hand, was an incalculable risk: if Mohammadu noticed that I was pregnant after our "marriage"—which would inevitably happen in my current condition—he would feel I had deceived him, and he would want to take his revenge. He might take advice from the imam. I hadn't forgotten the sight of the woman who had bled to death in Kauri after her belly had been slit open—and I was sure that that would be my fate and the fate of my child if I dared to deceive him. No, marriage wasn't a solution anymore. Perhaps I should have gone for it earlier, but now the moment had passed. I had hesitated for too long.

One morning Mohammadu was suddenly standing outside the gate of the compound. His superiors had assigned him and two other men to guard us during the day and go with us to our religious studies classes. Soon our group was walking together down the long path past the farms and fields to the school building.

I avoided looking at Mohammadu on our march. But I immediately noticed that he wanted to talk to me. Eventually, when we were halfway there, he was suddenly walking beside me. "Have you changed your mind?" he asked.

I barely dared to say no, so I didn't say anything at all. He understood my answer anyway. "So you haven't," he said.

"I can't. Would you want to marry an adulteress?"

"Your loyalty to your husband is an honor to you," he said. It sounded half mocking, half genuine. "I just hope you know what you're doing." He edged closer to me and looked around to check that no one was listening to us. Then he said quietly, "You've got to get married anyway. If you don't marry me, then marry someone else. No woman who refuses will be left alive. Do you understand?"

I looked at him in alarm. Did he want to threaten me now?

"We'll kill you all," he said seriously. "So if you really don't want to get married, I urgently advise you to get as far away from here as possible."

# Shattered dreams

Renate blanches when I tell her about my last conversation with Patience. "Boko Haram has occupied Gavva?" she asks, unable to grasp what I've told her.

She knew that Boko Haram was active in the area, and had attacked the church in 2013. But now I'm confirming her worst suspicions about the tragedy that's being played out there. "Yes, they've taken Gavva," I say, passing on Patience's report to Gavva's former missionary. "They have turned the village into a concentration camp. All the people who didn't manage to escape are being kept there as slaves. The men are forced to work, the boys are made into holy warriors and the women and girls become 'wives' to the fighters as soon as they are forced into marriage."

Renate is frozen with horror. "Our village—a camp!" she says over and over again. "How could that happen?" She looks into the sky, almost as if she is angry with her God.

But she doesn't utter a word of criticism, just a sigh. "And my house?" she asks. "The mission station?"

I don't want to answer, but she'll find out anyway. "Patience says Boko Haram people live there now. She saw them in the garden."

"For heaven's sake!" she says. "The beautiful garden I loved. I don't want to imagine what's happening there."

Renate is completely beside herself. She is deeply shaken by the tragedy that is playing out in the place where she once lived. She thinks about the people she knew there, and wonders which of them managed to escape in time. She has seen some of them in Maiduguri. And what about the rest of the congregation?

"I feel so sorry for the people who are being humiliated and tortured in the camp," she keeps saying. "It's so unfair. They always tried to make life better. And so did I." She can't come to terms with the fact that the disaster seems to mean the end of all her endeavors. She did so much there. Was it all in vain?

The vicar wants to know more about the situation in Gavva. She systematically begins questioning people who might be able to tell her something. First she talks to her closest colleague, Rebecca from Ngoshe. But Rebecca left the area just in time, and hence too quickly to be able to give any reliable information on what had happened in the meantime.

"We haven't had telephone contact with the villages for ages, either with Ngoshe or Gavva," she says. "Boko Haram destroyed the towers."

"Yes, I know that," Renate says impatiently. "But what do the women who have come from there report?"

"I've stopped asking them," she admits. "What I know already is quite enough. I don't want to hear anything more."

Renate shakes her head disapprovingly. But the fact is that the women who have escaped the horror are only willing to reveal a little of what they have seen or experienced. The memories are too unpleasant to share. And they make people feel ashamed. The only thing they are willing to discuss is the whereabouts of relatives.

The same is true in Renate's workshops. When the widows come to the church compound to be initiated into the mysteries of soap-making, or to bake muffins together, they focus strictly on the task at hand: they eye the ingredients curiously, talk about their prices and listen closely as the individual steps of the manufacturing process are explained. The ones who can write record the recipes that Renate gives them. And when the pieces of soap are laid in the sun to dry and the first self-baked goods are being tasted, the women's conversations revolve around things close to home: their accommodations, their children, the various ways of earning money. But none of them willingly talks about their own story. They each keep their pain to themselves.

Renate is now terribly anxious about the situation in Gavva. On the spur of the moment she asks Daniel to come with her to a refugee camp where some women from Gavva live. It is right next to our church compound. I go with them.

As a journalist I've already seen various refugee camps: in Iran, in Iraq, in Pakistan, even in Mali. And I actually thought that nothing could shock me in this respect. But the Nigerian camp goes beyond anything my jaded eye has ever seen. An incredible number of people are crammed into a tiny space. They sit on the floor, cook, eat, sleep, flick the flies away. You look in vain for white UN tents, only the camp management has one. The rest of the people are living in wooden shacks they've nailed together themselves, or under plastic sheets. Everything is incredibly dirty, and the impression it makes on me is of how squalid conditions are.

We step into the camp, and it isn't long before we are recognized. "*Bature, bature*—white woman!" the children shout. "You're the vicar," an elderly woman says to Renate. She is one of the ones who took part in the literacy program. Renate doesn't know her personally, but the woman greets her as if they were old friends.

"Which village do you come from?" Renate asks her.

The woman names a little village near Pulka.

"Do you know where I can find people from Gavva?"

"Oh, yes." She guides us to a group of women sharing one of the shacks made of plastic sheets. They too give Renate a warm welcome. They think highly of the vicar for not forgetting them in their misery.

In fact it's an important sign. So far no representative of the mission in Maiduguri has paid the refugees a visit—let alone offered them help. Since the mission station in Gavva was officially closed in 2004 the program is considered to have been wound down by its Swiss headquarters. Only Renate, who came here as a private individual, seems to be interested in the incalculable suffering of the people here.

"What's happening in Gavva?" is her burning question. "Is it true that our lovely village has been turned into a prison camp?"

"Yes, that's true," a woman tells her. "I was there myself and saw it with my own eyes. I escaped from there."

"How long ago was that?" I ask.

The woman looks uncertain; measurements of time are difficult in Africa. "About two months," she guesses. According to the others, she's the last one to have seen her home village at close quarters.

Nobody really knows if Boko Haram is still occupying the town. The women don't agree: some are inclined to believe the army, which is spreading optimistic reports. Others are skeptical. Still others suspect that the fighters can't be far away. "I've heard that they're holed up in the Mandara Mountains," one woman says.

Many of them can confirm Patience's horrific account. And also that all the women in Gavva have been forced into marriage. "My daughter is living with a man like that now," says a middle-aged woman. "She has a baby with him and she can't run away anymore."

"And the mission house I lived in?" Renate asks. "Is it still standing?"

"Yes, it is. But recently the Boko Haram fighters lived in it. They're using it as their headquarters for the valley."

The vicar lowers her head. Now she feels exactly like all the others: she really doesn't want to hear these terrible things. But she forces herself. She asks questions all afternoon and the women tell her more and more dreadful details about the practices of the sect.

One recurring motif in their accounts is the fetishism with which the group regards the blood of their victims. It isn't unlikely that these are African rituals with their roots in black magic. Because everyone here knows that the life-spirits of an adversary who has been killed pass to those who drink his blood or eat his organs. The practice is ancient. That is how a warrior symbolically absorbs the strength of his opponent.

The intimidating power of the demonstration of such practices should not be underestimated. Many Nigerians assume that the fighters—and principally their leader, Shekau—have magical powers that make them immune to army attacks. The sect was even said to have protected the access routes to the Sambisa Forest, Boko Haram's place of retreat, with a magic spell. The people had no other way of understanding how the terrorist leader had managed to hole up in swampland a couple hundred square miles in area. Presumably the legends formed around Boko Haram are deliberately fed and provoked to win respect and keep the population in a constant state of fear. Neither politicians nor the army, which should in fact be fighting Boko Haram, are entirely free from this.

The women suffer from all this. The ones whose husbands have been cut down in front of their eyes, and the ones who have survived the horror of being taken prisoner. The worst, they report, is the feeling of helplessness "when you are left at the mercy of these bad people and there's nothing you can do." Traumatology teaches us that these terrible impressions will pursue them throughout their whole lives. And the feeling of impotence will stay with them.

When we leave the women, my sixty-five-year-old companion is shattered. The women's accounts have realized her worst fears: Boko Haram, Renate is forced to admit, have destroyed her life's work.

That may not be easy to accept. I can see the state that Renate is in. Perhaps she is wondering why she should set up anything at all here, if men then come and destroy everything again. She walks restlessly back and forth in the church courtyard. She talks to Rebecca, discussing what can be done. But the vicar is just as powerless with regard to the violence as the rest of us are.

"Perhaps we'll soon be able to build everything back up in Gavva again," Rebecca tries to comfort her, but she doesn't seem to believe her own words. Because like everyone in Maiduguri she knows that going back in the near future will still be far too dangerous.

We have seen what can happen when the fragile equilibrium between the tribes is destroyed—in Gubla, for example, a majority Muslim town near the villages of Sukur with their traditional beliefs. After being liberated by the army, the people of Sukur carried out an unbelievable massacre, Renate tells me: they accused the Muslims of cooperating with Boko Haram and invading their land. The people of Sukur even killed 150 young men of their own tribe, accusing them of being traitors.

The same might also happen in the area around Gavva: wherever the population follows different religions and the suspicion of cooperating with the murderers is in the air, retaliation can follow. Retaliation that leads to further revenge.

In our room in the evening Renate says to me: "The women can't go back to our valley. Even if Boko Haram leaves them alone, there will be no peace there for a long time."

I agree with her. Gavva and the whole Gwoza district were at the center of a reign of terror. It will probably be years before normal life is possible there again. But what is the alternative? Maiduguri is bursting at the seams, and it's hard to build up a new material existence here. And relations between Christians and Muslims in the city are more tense than they have recently been. "It could be a long time before the situation here in the north calms down a little."

"Maybe they should be taken to a different part of the country." Renate looks at me searchingly. "What do you think of that idea?"

"What do you mean exactly?"

"Well, buying a piece of land further south! A piece of land where the widows can build their houses and work."

I bring my hands to my head. "Sounds good!" I say spontaneously. I don't need to think for long.

"I've got twenty thousand euros at most; that might buy me a plot of land in Jos," she says.

Now I can tell that the idea wasn't as spontaneous as it seemed at first. Renate has quite concrete plans. Apparently she has been considering the idea of buying land for quite some time.

"No man can set foot on that land," she says. "Not even a guard. They will have to learn to defend themselves."

That can't do any harm. But why is Renate being so severe, I wonder, and ask her.

"Because he would immediately tell the women what to do," the vicar explains. "That's just how the culture is. Even if he's just employed as a caretaker, within a very short time he'll be in charge." She wants to prevent that. All the more so given the brutal violence that many of the women have experienced from men. I begin to see her argument.

"So, a kind of commune. A new home for the widows and their children." It's a brilliant idea, I think. Can there be a more permanent form of development aid than buying a patch of land for the women and making them its owners? They might be able to escape their terror in Jos.

And then I think of Patience: how beautiful it would be if she got a place there too—and could finally leave Maiduguri with her baby. I hope the project comes into being!

But Renate is curiously confident. She closes her eyes and seems to be consulting her contacts on high.

# Reunion abroad

Mohammadu's words made me shudder. But I was sure he was telling the truth. Sooner or later the fighters killed everyone for whom they had no use.

I battled with myself over whether I should trust him. Could I risk telling him about my actual problem? In the end I gave myself a shove: I had to take the risk.

"I'm pregnant," I confessed.

He looked at my belly. "Of course! Why didn't I notice that?" he said at last. "It explains a lot."

"What should I do?"

"You need to get away from here right now."

"Will you help me?"

He said nothing for a long time. "You're asking a lot."

"You could let me escape on the way to school," I suggested.

"Are you crazy?" he whispered furiously. "You must think I'm tired of life!"

We spoke no more that day. In the evening, when I went to bed among the other women, I brooded for a long time about whether I had done the right thing—and I was racked with doubts. Had I been over-hasty in revealing my secret to one of the fighters? How could I dare to trust him? Just because he didn't seem quite as reckless as his comrades?

Now I was at his mercy. No, *we* were at his mercy. "Don't let him use our secret against us," I asked God in my prayers that night. "Save us as you have done before!"

Some days passed. Mohammadu and I didn't exchange a word. When he walked us to school he no longer tried to be near me. It was as if our conversation had never happened. Eventually I really thought he had forgotten it. Should I be disappointed? Or relieved? It mightn't be the worst thing that could happen, I thought in a mixture of the two emotions: I'd probably just asked too much of him. I understood that he couldn't let me escape, his comrades would inevitably have made him take the consequences. And I knew what they did to men who deliberately missed when shooting. No one who was fond of life could risk that.

The more I thought about it, the more foolish my request seemed to me. It had been ludicrous to imagine that he would fulfill it. Only I could take that risk. And perhaps I would have to accept death as the possible consequence.

In the evening men came to our compound again to choose women for themselves. Mohammadu wasn't one of them. But his colleagues showed a growing interest in me. If one of them looked at me, I broke out in a cold sweat. Things wouldn't go well for long, I knew. When would one of them take me? Or discover my pregnant belly? I was surprised that it hadn't happened already. Were they blind? My life hung on a silk thread. I definitely had to do something, or my child and I would surely die.

On one of the following evenings Mohammadu came through the gate to the compound. I was very surprised to see him. It looked as if he too was in search of a bride. I secretly watched him and his friends walking along the rows, making lewd remarks about some of the women. They seemed to be having a great time.

Then they came to me. "Well, you're still here, does no one want you?" Mohammadu said loudly. The other men laughed.

I looked at him sadly. Was he mocking me too now? Was he laughing at my plight? "I wouldn't take that one with the flat face either," he said to his friends.

Then they moved on. The men were already focused on the next woman. Then Mohammadu turned back to me. "During the *tahajjud* prayer the compound is unguarded," he whispered to me.

At first I was far too startled to understand what he had just said. It was probably just as well. Because before I could reply he was back with his comrades, and they were continuing with their game.

When they left our compound, three of them had chosen new "wives."

Mohammadu glanced at me once more before he left. His face was completely blank. I didn't show any emotion either. But I wanted to run after him and kiss his feet.

*

My heart pounded strangely when the sun went down. The compound became quieter. But I was wondering how I could keep from getting tired. I couldn't afford to miss the *tahajjud* prayer.

This prayer isn't one of the five obligatory Muslim prayers that Boko Haram made us women perform every day. It was, you might say, an extra prayer that only very pious people prayed, and happened some time in the middle of the night. Sometimes I heard the call of the prayer leader, and we women just went on sleeping. But the two guards who kept watch over our prison at night clearly took things more seriously. It had never occurred to me that they would simply leave us unguarded for those ten minutes.

But if I interpreted Mohammadu's words correctly, that was exactly what happened. What an incredible stroke of luck! I gauged the height of the mud wall surrounding our prison. Would it be possible to climb it? I would have to lift myself up with my arms, or ... Or I needed someone to help me. Should I tell one of the women of my plans? I couldn't tell too many, or our intentions would be in jeopardy.

I looked around at my fellow prisoners. I wasn't particularly close to any of them. But Lami Ali, a stout little woman in her mid-twenties, had always been nice to me. Unasked, she had made it her duty to ensure that I got a portion when the food was being handed out. She had been a mother several times over, and had been the only member of her family of seven who had stayed behind in Gavva because she hadn't been able to run fast enough when Boko Haram came to the village. In my eyes that made her a fellow sufferer.

"Lami Ali," I said, drawing her gently toward the edge of the compound so that the other women couldn't hear us.

"Yes, what is it?"

I took a deep breath. "I'm running away tonight," I told her. Her eyes widened. She looked anxiously around. "Are you coming?"

"But how are you going to do that?"

"The compound is unguarded during the *tahajjud* prayer."

"How do you know that?"

"It doesn't matter."

"No, it does. Our lives depend on it."

I understood that she needed to know what she was getting involved in. "One of them told me."

"It could be a trap," she said.

"No, I believe him. I think he wants to help me."

Understandably enough, Lami Ali was very suspicious. She gave me lots of reasons why we shouldn't risk it. But of course she hoped that I would contradict them all. "If you stay here, you'll get married," I warned her. "Then you'll never be able to see your husband again."

At last I managed to convince her. "OK," she said at last. "I'm in."

I gave her a huge hug.

Gradually all the women withdrew into the huts and lay down on the floor. We found a place among them right near the door. Soon we heard the quiet snores of the other women, who had gone to sleep straightaway, exhausted by the exertions of the day. But we were desperate not to fall asleep, so we had come up with a system. At regular intervals we would pinch and shake each other.

That worked quite well for a while. I kept reaching out a hand toward my accomplice and she did the same thing. But I slowly realized that my hand was growing heavier and the intervals were getting longer. I listened to the noises of the night to distract myself and keep from drifting off into the world of dreams.

Eventually I gave a start. Had I gone to sleep? I could tell from Lami Ali's regular breathing that she had nodded off as well. What time was it? Had I already missed the call to prayer? I was annoyed, because I had completely lost my sense of time.

Alarmed by my oversight, I sat up and forced myself to remember hymns. I tried to call their tunes to mind, and go through the words in my mind. But even using that trick it was difficult not to doze off again. At last I heard the prayer leader's call, drifting over the village at night with its sing-song chant.

I immediately shook my companion awake. "Come on, it's time," I whispered.

She rubbed her eyes drowsily. Then all of a sudden, she was wide awake. Very carefully and in silence, we tiptoed around the other bodies that lay stretched out on the floor. One false step and we would have woken the whole group. Then we were standing outside. I breathed in the fresh, cool night air; it was delicious, like a harbinger of freedom.

I listened for the voices of the guards. But everything seemed to be quiet. We were about to make our way to the mud wall when I heard a sound in the hut. My heart almost stopped with fear. The outline of a woman had appeared in the doorway to the hut. I recognized her straightaway: it was Blessing. A shy young woman who sometimes looked a little clumsy and awkward, perhaps because she was so tall. People whispered behind their hands that she was pregnant too—by a fighter. But of course it was only rumors.

"What are you two doing?" she asked.

"Nothing," I said. What else was I supposed to say? I struggled to explain our nocturnal outing. "I wanted to go to the toilet and Lami ... "

"Are you escaping?" said Blessing. "Will you take me with you?" It sounded like a plea.

Lami Ali and I exchanged a look. "Of course you're coming too," I whispered. "But hurry up. We haven't much time."

We walked behind the hut to the wall, which was about six feet high. You had to make a bit of an effort to climb it, but it wasn't impossible. That was why it was usually guarded.

First of all, they helped me climb to the top: I stepped on Lami Ali's knee, then Blessing pushed my bottom up. It was all quite simple. I sat at the top of the wall. Next Blessing crouched down and Lami Ali stood on her shoulders. Then the tall girl stood up. And since she was a giantess, she was able to get her to the edge without much difficulty. I helped Lami Ali to the top. And at last, when we were both on top of the wall—and with one foot in freedom—we somehow had to pull Blessing up as well. Of course that was a bit more difficult, because there was nothing down there that she could use as a support. And we were now all quite nervous, because the prayer had just finished, which meant that our guards could come back at any moment.

Blessing started feeling guilty, as she didn't want to jeopardise our flight. "Just run, I'll be fine," she said, trying to drag herself up. But I knew she wouldn't be able to do it all by herself.

"Take our hands," I said to her. "We'll pull you up."

She didn't seem to be able to imagine it. "No, run," she wailed.

"Take our hands and shut up," I told her.

Lami Ali grabbed one of her hands and her forearm, I took the other. Together we finally managed to bring her to the top. Then we heard the men chatting as they came back from their prayer. Damn!

"Should we go back?" Lami Ali whispered.

"No! I'm not going back!" I said firmly.

"Neither am I," Blessing agreed.

"Then let's go!"

We jumped from the wall into the darkness, and landed in a stony field. The impact was so loud that the guards in the gateway heard it. I lost my slippers as we came down.

"Hey, what was that?" one of the men asked his colleagues.

"No idea. An animal?"

"I'm going to take a look."

He shone a torch toward us, but didn't spot us straightaway. But he was still trudging in our direction. Meanwhile, we pulled ourselves up and ran off. I was barefoot. We hurried as quickly as we could across a dark field within the village.

"Hey, you there!" the man behind us shouted. "Stop right now!" I heard gunshots ringing out in the night. The man was shooting at us, or at least trying to. But in the darkness he didn't know exactly where to aim, so he missed.

"Ignore him, keep going!" I told my two fellow escapees.

We hurried along the dark paths of Gavva. The guard stumbled along behind us. His gunfire made a lot of noise that brought other fighters running as well. But since there was no light anywhere neither he nor any of the others managed to hit us.

Eventually the shots fell silent. We had left the settlement behind us—and apparently our pursuers as well. At any rate, we couldn't hear them anymore. We still went on running, now across the fields. But we weren't really sure in which direction we were headed.

Blessing was the first to show signs of exhaustion. "I can't go on," she panted. "You keep going without me."

"Not far now," I encouraged her, and she summoned her strength again. We ran on.

We didn't take a break until we were quite sure that we had lost the men. We were panting like hunted animals. But we were incredibly happy that our daring plan had actually worked. Lami Ali, and Blessing in particular, started crying loudly.

"Are you crazy? Stop that right now!" I said to them. Startled, they tried to control themselves. But after everything we'd been through they found it very difficult. The relief was too great. Meanwhile I maintained my composure. I didn't trust the peace. After all, I had already believed once before that I had escaped Boko Haram, and I knew that the feeling might be deceptive.

"We're not safe yet," I told my companions. "Don't forget that Boko Haram are everywhere around here."

They looked around uneasily. "Where are we?" Lami Ali asked. It was hard in the darkness to make out any distinctive features. The landscape, the fields scattered with trees that ran along either side of the village, looked pretty much the same even during the day. But at night everything seemed to blur together. However, I had a sense that the sky was slightly brighter on one side than on the other. Perhaps the sun was rising over there, which meant that was the east—and on the other side were the mountains. Or had the moon just set over there? It was quite confusing.

"The mountains are over there," Blessing said as if reading my mind. She pointed toward the darkest part of the night sky.

"How do you know that?" I asked her.

"I know that tree there." She pointed at a dark outline. "My brother often used to rest there with his goats when he was going into the mountain."

"So we've been heading westward."

"Then let's carry on in this direction," said Lami Ali. "We may be able to get to the mountains before the sun comes up."

But I voiced my concern. "Are you crazy? The mountains are a blind alley. I've been trapped there before." I told them about how the men had encircled us and caught us in the net. "I'm not going back up there."

"But the road and Gwoza are on the other side!"

"There's no safety in Gwoza either: I've seen with my own eyes that it's been occupied."

Shocked, my companions said nothing. They had known that Boko Haram had taken over smaller villages in the area, but not that the group controlled the district capital. "But we can't stay here waiting in the fields," they said in despair.

"We've got to turn round and head toward Cameroon." I pointed into the mountains to the east, in the other direction.

"But we can't go back to Gavva!" Blessing objected.

"We don't want to go there either. We have to skirt the town."

"Patience is right," said Lami Ali. "We'll only be safe from them on the other side of the border."

"How far is it from here to Cameroon?" asked Blessing. "Can we get there before it's light?"

I didn't know. "I don't think so, but the earlier we get going the better. So let's not waste any more time," I said.

In the end I managed to persuade them. So we turned around and walked back in the direction we had come from. Of course we gave Gavva a wide berth: luckily Blessing and Lami Ali knew the secret paths. But it wasn't easy to keep our bearings, because we weren't walking along roads, but marching across the fields.

At dawn we had left the village that was now a prison camp behind us again, on the other side this time. But we were still very frightened at the idea of coming across a checkpoint or one of their patrols. And the lighter it grew, and the closer we came to the border, the more nervous we became.

"Perhaps we should hide somewhere and only set off again in the evening," Lami Ali said.

"When we're so close to our destination?" I looked around. Yes, she was right, I thought: we couldn't afford to be frivolous. But where, for heaven's sake, should we hide?

So we decided to go on a little further and see if we could find a decent hiding place. Even the few trees and bushes didn't really give us protection. We weren't sure how far we still had to walk, and felt very tired. But we didn't dare to lie down and sleep anywhere: anyone passing by would inevitably find us.

By now it was morning. The sun was hot, and almost vertical in the sky. It was getting more and more dangerous to go on walking. But we couldn't stop either. So we kept on walking straight through the bush. I had a silent conversation with my God: "Father, don't let them find us," I begged. "Please don't do it to me again. I and my child and the other women have suffered enough!"

Eventually we reached the river, which I knew marked the border between the two countries. It was the same one that flowed beyond Ashigashiya—or didn't flow. Because normally it was, as I have said, dry. But now, so soon after the rainy season, it was a stream.

"This is the end of Nigeria," I said to the others. "Cameroon is over there."

They looked around suspiciously. I could understand what was happening in their heads. This stream in the middle of nowhere really didn't look like a national border. There was no checkpoint, no barbed wire. Not so much as a flag waved on the other side.

"Are you quite sure?" Blessing asked dubiously.

"Yes," I reassured her.

Lami Ali was the first to believe me: "That means we're at our destination," she whooped, "thanks be to God in heaven!" She was about to fall on her knees and utter a prayer of thanks, but I held her back.

"First let's wade to the other side. OK?"

"All right, then," she agreed. She too was concerned that it might be risky. So they both took off their rubber sandals—I had been walking barefoot since we jumped over the wall—and we rolled up our skirts. Then we crossed the little river.

It was only when we reached the other side that we fell into each other's arms. Now we were sure of it: we had really done it.

We went on walking on the other side of the border. The landscape barely changed. If I hadn't known that Cameroon was on that side of the river, I wouldn't have noticed that we had entered another country. There was just less agriculture here, fewer harvested fields. We were surrounded mostly by typical bushland with its wild grasses and scrub. The vegetation was the same as it was in Nigeria.

I can't remember how long it was before we reached a road. Did we dare to walk along it? If we had crossed the border so easily, then the Boko Haram fighters could do the same. And who could give us a guarantee that they weren't active on this side of the border? On the other hand, the march through the bush was very difficult, and we were gradually becoming exhausted. We couldn't wander around in the wilderness forever.

"Let's take the road," I suggested to my companions, "it's bound to bring us to a village."

"Isn't that too dangerous?" Blessing asked. "What if the village is occupied?"

I wasn't sure myself. But did we have another choice? We urgently needed a resting place, water and food. Somewhere we had to find people that we could ask for help.

While we stood there thinking about what to do, we heard voices nearby. Startled, we took refuge behind a big tree a little way from the road. Were they Boko Haram people? Or border soldiers who would send us back? We waited tensely as the voices came ever closer.

Then we saw them: a group of ragged figures walking along the road. They were men, about half a dozen. But they didn't look like Boko Haram fighters, more like farmers—or ex-farmers. They looked poor and gaunt, and their clothes were ragged. Perhaps they had escaped as well? We were very curious. We would have liked to talk to them and ask where they had come from, but didn't dare to draw attention to ourselves.

We waited until they'd passed. Then we dared to come out of hiding and follow them at an appropriate distance. Perhaps they would lead us to a village where normal people lived, we thought.

We soon discovered that they had a different goal. It was further on, away from the road: hundreds of people were camping in the wilderness, clearly refugees like us. But they weren't in tents, they had set up their camp on the bare ground. Some of them didn't even have a mat on which they could sleep or sit.

It was a strange sight, so many wretched, half-starving people all at once. They came, we soon discovered, from our home, from Gavva, Ngoshe, Pulka and the other villages of the Gwoza district that Boko Haram had attacked and occupied. They had probably run full pelt and then become stranded here, just beyond the border, because they couldn't afford to travel on. It broke my heart to see my fellow countrymen like that. But I secretly hoped: perhaps I would find my family here again?

My companions had already discovered the first familiar faces in the crowd—and the people there had discovered us. "Mama!" cried a little boy and ran up to Lami Ali. Her whole face beamed when she picked up her little son. He covered her face with kisses. And then still more children came, all clearly hers. "What took you so long?" an older girl complained to her mother. "We thought you weren't coming back."

Lami Ali began to sob. "I would have been with you much sooner," she assured her children. "But I couldn't. I've missed you very much."

Blessing and I watched her and her children for a while, then we left too, to go in search of our own families. I wondered anxiously whether Ishaku had managed to get here. How lovely it would be to spot his face among all these strangers.

A middle-aged man now came up to Blessing. He didn't look very friendly, but she still seemed pleased to see him. "Father!" she cried. She hurried toward him and tried to hug him, but he kept her at a distance.

"Where have you been?" he asked reproachfully.

"In Gavva. I was taken prisoner."

"Nothing happened to you?" he asked. "I mean ... " He looked her contemptuously up and down.

"No, Father. It's all fine," she reassured him and looked at me despairingly. I quickly took my leave.

Now I was suddenly all alone among these people. No one paid me any attention. It was as if everyone was preoccupied with themselves and their own families. The camp was like a big village, except that there were no walls. Everything that people did—eating, sleeping, cooking or washing their clothes—they did in the open, and in front of everyone. They seemed to have got used to it. They didn't notice one more strange face among the many faces around them. At least that was how it seemed to me as I wandered among the people who were lounging about here. I noticed that the heat and the exhaustion were slowly making me feel dizzy. What would I do if I didn't find anyone from my family? Would anyone help me?

On the ground, beside the mats of a large family, I saw a canister of water. The mother, a tall, plump woman, kept filling little cups and giving them to her children. I felt terribly thirsty. Where had she got that water from? Could I ask her for a sip?

Because I didn't dare speak to her, I looked around for a well. But of course there wasn't one out here. They must have got hold of it somewhere else.

Then I suddenly felt someone tugging at my skirt. It was a little boy with bright eyes and a lot of dust in his hair. I had to look at him twice, but then I recognized him: it was my husband's oldest son. "Yoshua," I cried with delight and picked him up. "Are your parents and brother and sister here too?"

He nodded shyly.

"Where?" I asked excitedly. "Can you take me to them?"

"Yes, of course."

Yoshua ran on ahead. I could see that he was already very familiar with the camp. He guided me resolutely through the sea of people and mats. Then he suddenly stopped by the back of a man sitting on the ground in the shade of a big tree.

"Patience is here, Dad!" said Yoshua.

The man turned round. It was Ishaku. When he saw me, he clearly thought he was seeing a ghost from the past. At any rate he didn't speak a word of greeting.

But I burst into tears of joy and relief.

# Dying and living

My husband ignored me. I think that was the shock. Now he had lost me and found me again for the second time. He couldn't cope with it. Or perhaps he thought I was playing some sort of game to surprise him.

He didn't say a word to me all day. Lara treated me with the same indifference with which she had always treated me since I burst into their lives unexpectedly. She had probably thought she was rid of me once and for all, and wasn't particularly pleased that I'd managed to escape again. But she pulled herself together. She gave me something to drink, and let me sit with them.

Her three children gave me the warmest greeting. Little Tabita in particular was very pleased to see me: she climbed into my lap—and immediately noticed the swelling in my belly, which didn't match my otherwise gaunt body. She rested her little hands on the spherical shape, which probably felt very hard. I didn't think she had any idea what was hidden behind it. In her eyes the swelling was probably just something new. Her mother looked at both of us with suspicion.

The two boys skipped excitedly around me. Yoshua soon lost his initial shyness and fired questions at me. "Where have you been, Patience?" he wanted to know. "Why didn't you come with us?"

I smiled sadly. "I would have loved to," I said. "But bad men took me prisoner and kept me there."

He looked at me wide-eyed. "What sort of men?" he asked. "What did they do with you?"

"Well, you can see the answer to that one," Lara muttered under her breath.

I ignored her. But her remark made me very nervous. What sort of unpleasant game was she playing? Was she going to persuade Ishaku that the child wasn't his? She knew I was pregnant before I was abducted the first time.

Ishaku had clearly heard her words as well. He glanced at my belly and only now did he seem to notice my condition. But I didn't say a word.

My family had already made themselves reasonably comfortable in the makeshift camp, and they owned a few of the things needed for daily life: mats for sleeping on, a few blankets and cloths, a piece of soap, a sack of millet, a bottle of groundnut oil and a wood-burning stove, for instance. I didn't know exactly where our modest equipment came from. But I assumed that Ishaku had bought it. Perhaps he had managed to take some money with him when he escaped, after all. He wouldn't have told me or Lara in any case, because we might have started making demands on him. Money is a subject that African men prefer to keep from their wives.

On the wood-burning stove Lara prepared dinner for us. The pot of millet smelled delicious as ever, and reminded me of the first few months of our marriage. It seemed to be a long time ago. She gave me a small portion as well, and I devoured it hungrily.

After that there wasn't much to do in the camp. The men sat together in groups and chatted. The women cleaned the cooking pots and looked after the children. Then they all lay down on the mats. Of course I didn't have one of my own, so I just lay on the ground.

When it was dark, Ishaku came to me. He brought me a sheet to wrap myself in. But he made it clear that he was only doing it out of duty.

At last he broke his silence. "What sort of stories are these, Patience?" he demanded to know. "How could you let those people catch you again? Wasn't once enough?"

I couldn't believe that he was throwing accusations at me. "I couldn't help it," I said in self-defense. "They put down nets. Didn't you see that?"

"Did that man have anything to do with it?"

"Which man?"

"The one I caught you with in the field."

He meant Petrus. The whites of his eyes gleamed in the dark as he gave me a hostile look. "I should—" He raised his hand. I ducked out of the way, because I was afraid he wanted to hit me. But he lowered his arm again.

"He has nothing to do with it. He saved me," I implored him.

"You've told me that before," he said. "But why did he take you prisoner again—because he got you pregnant, is that it?"

"Do you mean that?"

"Of course I mean it. What husband wouldn't be interested in what his wife is doing with a strange man?"

I didn't know what to say. Ishaku's accusations were so absurd that I was speechless. I started crying quietly. "I swear to God that it isn't so."

"Oh, really? Lara says . . . "

"Yes, of course she thinks something else! But it's a lie, she just wants to get rid of me!"

I had spoken quite loudly. Lara, who was sleeping only a few yards away, had probably heard every word. But it didn't matter: if she wanted to destroy my life, I had the right to defend myself even if she was the first wife and the older of the two of us.

"Psst, hold your tongue!" Ishaku raged. "Or do you want to wake the whole camp? Do you want everyone to hear what you've been up to? Is that what you want? To damage my reputation?"

His words sounded harsh. But I could feel quite clearly that I had made him uncertain. Ishaku liked me, I knew that. But now he was fighting with his pride as a husband. Lara doubtless wasn't the only one who told him these things. The whole camp was probably talking about us kidnapped girls—and imagining what the men had done to us. That meant that we were being abused twice: once by our abductors, and many more times in the heads of the people who talked about it for their own secret amusement. The mere thought repelled me. Yes, that was how it was, and there was nothing we could do about it, I thought bitterly.

"I told you I was pregnant before I was kidnapped," I reminded Ishaku.

"I know nothing about that."

"Then you've forgotten. It's your child! Believe me!" I pleaded with him.

"So no one touched you."

"No one," I lied.

For a while Ishaku said nothing. He was battling with himself. With the voices in his head that were whispering one thing to him, and the others whispering the opposite. I could practically listen in to them. I silently begged Jesus to make the gossiping tongues fall silent.

"In that case, fine," Ishaku said at last. "I trust you, Patience." He rested his hand on my belly. "So this is my child."

"Yes, your own flesh and blood," I confirmed.

I kissed him and he returned my kisses. I assume that Lara, lying on her mat, was biting her hand with fury to keep from shouting out loud when she heard us making peace that night. After that I belonged entirely to Ishaku. Once again.

Life in the camp in the middle of the bush made huge demands on the whole family. Every day was a new challenge to us, camping out under the open sky and taking charge of our everyday life there.

The children in particular suffered from being constantly exposed to the weather. Luckily the rainy season was over by now. But the harmattan caused us difficulties, the fine desert dust that blew in our direction from the Sahara and covered our bodies and our hair. We could all have done with a good wash.

And some good food. We were given basic food, chiefly grain, by the government of Cameroon. Every time the truck came there were fights among the men, who were all trying to grab hold of some food for their families from the new cargo. The canisters of water were also brought by truck, because the water from the half dried-up river nearby was undrinkable. It could be used at best for washing clothes. Either way, it wasn't enough: neither enough water nor enough food.

So Ishaku often walked with the other men to the nearest town to make some money as a day laborer. They loaded trucks, carried boxes around at the market, did some cleaning work or weeded the fields. They took any job they could get to improve our situation. Ishaku never told us what he earned. Usually he immediately converted it into something we could eat.

But one day he came back to us looking very pleased with himself. He was carrying a gourd that he had bought in the market. We would live on it for at least two days. That would have been reason enough to be happy, but Ishaku had something even better to report: he had charged his mobile phone and managed to speak to his mother.

That was actually good news, because we had heard that her village had also been attacked and occupied. We hadn't heard anything from Ishaku's family for a long time. "She's in Cameroon as well and living with my brother," he told us happily, and named a village perhaps twelve miles away.

"Oh, they're living in a village?" I asked. It sounded more comfortable than our life here.

"Yes," Ishaku said thoughtfully. His brother had probably rented some kind of lodging there. "They say they're fine."

"I'm glad," I said. I secretly hoped we would soon manage to escape our situation as well. Living without a roof over our head was becoming more and more difficult as my pregnancy advanced: by now I had quite a fat belly, and the heat was becoming a problem for me. But I was also concerned about the lack of hygiene. How could you look after a baby in this environment, if we didn't even have enough water to wash every day?

We had visitors a few days later. One late morning, when the sun was already quite high in the sky, suddenly a middle-aged lady appeared in front of us in the camp. She wore a freshly washed yellow and blue floral patterned dress, decent shoes and even bracelets around her wrists. Among all these dusty figures she was like a glowing apparition. But what struck me most about her was her face: her nose and eyes were startlingly like my husband's. This must be my mother-in-law.

I watched her going from family to family and talking to them in turn. She was obviously looking for us. I nudged Ishaku.

His eyes widened when he saw her. "I told her not to come," he murmured, before getting to his feet and hurrying toward her. "Mother!" he said to her with a mixture of joy and reproach. "What are you doing here?"

"My boy!" she cried, and performed a proper little dance of joy. "It's so good to see you!"

She hugged her son warmly. Now Lara was coming toward her with the children in tow. The mother-in-law was half out of her mind with joy. After Ishaku had told her on the phone where he was stranded, she must have got on the bus to come and visit us. "I just had to convince myself that you were all right," she said, and patted the children's cheeks. "Is everything all right? Do you have enough to eat?"

Lara greeted her mother-in-law almost submissively, with all the respect that was due to her. I stayed in the background. As we hadn't celebrated our marriage, I hadn't yet met Ishaku's mother. So I waited modestly to be introduced. But no introduction was forthcoming. Nobody seemed to be thinking about me at all.

Ishaku sat down on a mat with his mother. Lara brought them bananas that she had hastily begged from a neighboring family. "This is a terrible place," I heard Ishaku's mother say. "You can't stay here."

"I know," he said. "But at the moment it's all we have. We're glad to have come away with our lives. Perhaps the situation will calm down soon."

"Let's hope so," she said, and sighed. "But still, this is no place for children. I wish I could help you."

"Isn't there enough room for us where you live?" Ishaku ventured. "Just as an interim measure, I mean. Until we've found something else."

His mother thought for a moment. She seemed to be seriously considering his suggestion. I listened excitedly to hear what she would say. "Yes, you're right," she said at last. "I can't leave you here."

Ishaku beamed. And I too was delighted at the prospect that our life in the open might soon come to an end. "Shall we come with you now?" my husband asked.

She hesitated. "Your brother will understand," she said as if to herself.

"We won't take up very much room," Ishaku promised. "I'll tell the women to pack their things. Oh yes ... " He suddenly seemed to remember that his mother and I had never met. He called me over. "Do you know Patience?"

His mother looked rather disheartened. She looked me up and down. Her eye lingered for a long time on my pregnant belly. "Is that yours?" she asked disapprovingly.

"She's my wife."

"Lara is your wife."

"My *second* wife."

"She's staying here," his mother said sharply.

"But she's pregnant!"

"I can see that." She got up and walked around in a circle. "Why is it that you men can never control yourselves?" she scolded. "Wouldn't one wife have been enough for you? How, excuse me, am I going to explain that to your brother?"

Ishaku lowered his head like a naughty boy getting a telling-off. And to some extent that was what was happening. He became very meek: "I will work and reimburse him for any expenses," he promised.

But his mother wouldn't hear of it. "I'm taking Lara and the children with me," she decided. "You and your sweetheart can stay here."

"But Mother!" he protested.

"No backchat from you. Your brother hasn't got enough room for so many people. If you can get her pregnant, you'll be able to look after her, won't you?"

However much Ishaku begged and pleaded, his mother would not be swayed. She would only give shelter to Lara and her three grandchildren. When she said goodbye to us, she took the four of them with her. Ishaku looked glumly after them as they marched off along the road.

Then there was just the two of us, miraculously just the two of us, as I had always wished. No, I can't say that I was unhappy with his mother's decision: now at least I had my husband all to myself again.

Ishaku and I stayed in the bush. We lived in pitiful conditions, but somehow we got by. As often as he could, Ishaku took occasional work in the village. With the money he earned he bought oil, salt, vegetables or sometimes even eggs for us. He was always very proud when he could bring me something. And now that there were only two of us, it was usually enough.

When the sun grew hotter and hotter in the course of the dry season, he bought fabric in the market and used it to make an awning, which he supported on a structure of branches. It gave us the shade we needed. We slept under it at night, and I liked that because it was like a cave. "When we're back in Gwoza, I'll build us something better," Ishaku promised me. But I must admit that I wasn't dissatisfied with our makeshift solution.

By now my pregnancy was sometimes troublesome. It wasn't as easy as it had been for me to collect firewood or fetch water. Every journey took longer than usual, and left me thoroughly exhausted. It couldn't be long until my child came into the world.

I was always very curious about the little creature that had been with me for so long, surviving all the exertions that I had imposed on it. Would I bring a boy or a girl into the world? Either way, I knew it would be a very special person.

Ishaku treated me with great attention and affection. When we lay together at night, he often stroked my belly. Then I knew that he was looking forward to his child, and waiting impatiently for the birth. He had completely shed his initial suspicion: he acted as if I had never been away from him. And I too tried my very hardest to forget the bad period in my life.

But it wasn't as easy as that, because Boko Haram's horrific realm was only a few miles away from us, beyond the unguarded border. Again and again people managed to escape their reign of terror and join us at our camp. The new arrivals told us terrible stories about conditions at home. According to their accounts, Boko Haram had turned several villages like Gavva into prison camps. Some of them also told us about massacres of people who were no longer needed. Things were supposed to have been particularly bad in my home village of Ngoshe: the Christian inhabitants there had first been forced to dig graves. Then the men had been made to stand beside the graves and wait until they were beheaded, one after another. That was what we were told by survivors who had managed to escape.

These reports were particularly hurtful to me, as I had received no further signs of life from my family in Ngoshe. No one could tell me what had happened to my father and uncle, and whether my brothers and sisters were still alive. So I feared that they were among the victims.

Boko Haram's headquarters was based in Gwoza, we were told. That was where their leader Shekau was said to live, that madman who I had met at the very beginning of my abduction in Ashigashiya, when he delivered a speech to us. He had renamed the town "the seat of wisdom." He was said to rule the whole area like a warlord. In these circumstances, the idea of returning was of course completely impossible. It was hard for us to make any plans for the future.

But our greatest concern was that the terrorists would eventually cease to restrict themselves to Nigerian territory. They knew where we were. So what if they took it into their heads to pursue us all the way here? There were no Nigerian or Cameroonian soldiers to protect us if they decided to attack our camp.

People were well aware of that. And many of them were afraid, particularly since we were all unarmed. Ishaku had bought a knife with the money he sometimes earned. I used it when cooking. But would it be much use to us if it came to the crunch? What good would a kitchen knife be against machine guns and machetes?

A few times I talked to him about whether we should think about moving somewhere else. But the government of Cameroon didn't make it easy for us to head further into the interior of the country: the supplies of grain and water that we relied on so much were given only to refugees who stayed in the border zone. Anywhere else we would have been thrown back on our own devices, and would have had neither a place to sleep nor anything to eat. Since we had no papers we would also have been illegal immigrants.

"It's not such a bad thing to stay nearby," Ishaku said, introducing other reasons. "What would we do abroad? After all, when everything's over we want to get back to Gwoza as quickly as possible." In his mind, this was all very temporary. But I was becoming increasingly concerned, particularly about the impending birth. If we were soon to be a proper family, we would need a house, not an awning. And what would become of us in the rainy season?

"By the time the rainy season comes we'll have been at home for ages," he said. "After all, we have to tend to our field."

I looked at him doubtfully.

"This horror won't last forever, believe me," he said. "I've heard that the government is planning a major offensive to win the north back."

"I hope they do it soon."

"Yes, very soon," he said, firmly convinced.

*

I knew he was mistaken. Perhaps he knew it too and was only talking like that because he wanted to keep my spirits up. But conditions near the border were getting worse and worse. We heard of bombs going off in Cameroonian markets. There were lynchings wherever the refugees sought refuge. With their insatiable bloodlust, Boko Haram seemed actually to be following us into this neighboring country.

I was becoming more and more nervous. Perhaps my state of mind was down to the approaching end of my pregnancy. At any rate, I felt very unsafe so close to the border.

One night I was woken by faint noises. Even before I could work out what was happening, I noticed that metallic sound again, the sound of guns. I shook Ishaku awake.

"What's going on?" he asked.

"Something's happening in the camp," I whispered.

"Stay very calm, I'll go and check."

"No!" I begged. I didn't want to be left alone.

Then we heard the screams, screams of death. Within seconds I understood what was going on. The Islamists were attacking our camp.

"Run!" I said to Ishaku. "Quickly!"

I couldn't run myself. It was simply impossible in my condition. So soon before giving birth I felt as heavy and immobile as a hippopotamus. Ishaku didn't hesitate for a moment. But then he worked out that I had no chance of escaping.

"Look after our child," he whispered. And before I could say anything he was gone. He ran for his life with the others.

But I stayed lying where I was. I crept under my cloth and listened to the noise of the battle raging around me:

the trampling feet, the cries of *Allahu Akbar*, the shouting. Meanwhile I prayed quietly: "Lord, make me invisible. Keep your protecting hand over me and my child."

I was incredibly frightened. I lay there like that until morning. The noise gradually subsided. Eventually it grew lighter and I peered out from under the cloth. There was complete chaos all around me: mats, cloths, overturned wood-burning stoves and lost shoes lay scattered around on the ground. The whole area looked like a battlefield. In their panic the people had left behind everything that they owned. Behind a bush nearby I spotted a pair of legs lying motionless. I was filled with terror when I realized that the man lying there was dead. "Jesus!" I whispered.

When I looked more closely around, I saw more and more bodies lying motionless amid the chaos. Everyone who hadn't been able to run quickly enough had been either shot or beheaded. The place felt ghostly: apparently I was the only living soul who had been left here.

I didn't know what to do—and I didn't dare to go in any particular direction. Boko Haram people could still be nearby. So I just stayed there, under my cloth, and waited. I hope Ishaku will come back to me soon, I thought.

But he didn't come. In the course of the morning some people appeared in the camp. They were looking for their relatives, and calling out their names. Clearly Ishaku and I weren't the only ones who had lost one another amid all the confusion.

I asked everyone who came if they had seen my husband anywhere. But nobody could tell me anything. At last I went in search of him myself. I searched the bush, which was filled with traces of the previous night's flight: flattened grass, broken branches, sometimes a shoe that someone had lost while running. But worst of all were the corpses, which you suddenly stumbled over in the most unexpected places. It was a very strange sensation. As the day progressed and the sun did its work, they began to rot, and you could smell them even in the distance. I barely dared to go over and look at them: I was terrified that one of them might be Ishaku.

I moved further and further away from our camp. There was no sign of Ishaku. Eventually I bumped into a group of men who were also scouring the bush. I had seen Ishaku with some of them before; they had gone to the village together to ask for work. I asked them if they had any idea where he was. They looked at each other meaningfully. For a long time none of them said a word.

"What's happened to him?" I urged. "I'm his wife. I need to know."

One of them cleared his throat. "He's back there," he said.

"Where?"

"There, behind the trees." He pointed toward a place behind a clump of trees where some people had gathered.

Without even thanking the men I hurried away. As I did so I kept a look out for Ishaku. But I couldn't see him anywhere. As I got closer I noticed that the people were all strangers. They gave me an odd look as I hurried toward them. And then once more I smelled that strangely unpleasant smell, the smell of death. "I'm looking for my husband!" I said.

"Do you mean one of these?"

They pointed to the grass. Seven men's bodies lay there—and their severed heads. I stifled a scream when I saw Ishaku among them. First of all I recognized his clothes, the shirt and the trousers that he always wore. His head was slightly further away, to the side. I thought I was going mad when I saw him—and he seemed to look at me. No one had closed his eyes. His empty, lifeless gaze penetrated my soul. I will never forget him for as long as I live.

I can't say with any certainty what happened next. I was probably too shocked. I felt as if time had stood still.

I can remember only a small amount. I see Ishaku's head and the knife I found beside him in the grass: the tool of the killer, who had probably thrown it away after his work was done, or lost it when his people had beaten a hasty retreat. Before anyone could stop me I picked it up and hid it under my robes.

Otherwise I didn't see or hear anything else, the outside world had stopped existing. All the other people around me were just shadows whose words and gestures didn't reach me. I stood there completely alone.

Eventually they sent me away. The men who cleared the corpses didn't want us women to watch. So I left.

I wandered through the bush. I think I tried to find my way back to the camp. But I was too numb to do it. Tears kept pouring from my eyes, and my mind was in a state of utter confusion.

When I had completely lost my bearings I went into labor. The first pain hit me like a jolt, and dragged me back to reality.

It was like a wake-up call: with startling clarity I suddenly became aware of my situation. I was all alone in the wilderness. I couldn't bring a child into the world like this! "Not now!" I begged the little creature. But resistance was pointless: it had already made its decision long ago.

I stumbled forward. Perhaps I would make it back to the camp, where at least there were some women who could stay with me during the birth. But, as I said, I had no idea where to go, so I ended up going round in circles. The pains were getting more and more intense, and I had to sit down.

I was dizzy, and I was sweating all over. No, I wouldn't be able to walk anywhere at all, I knew suddenly, and became terribly frightened: no one would help me. I was left entirely alone with this difficult task ahead of me.

"Pull yourself together," I said to myself. "Other women have had children, after all." But I wasn't sure how the process worked. I had never been present to witness it. I'd heard the cries of the women, and also seen that they had a piece of wood put in their mouths so that they didn't make so much noise. Now I was slowly working out why they behaved like that. The pain was almost unbearable.

"You'll manage," I said to myself, trying to keep my spirits up. I *had* to do it. After all, I hadn't spent months hiding my child and protecting it from death for nothing. I had done that to give it life. This was the moment I had been yearning for. So giving up now was out of the question. Not least because the creature inside me didn't give me a choice: how could I have given it up? Even if I resisted, it was desperate to leave my body.

The pains were becoming unendurable. Soon the labor pains that I had felt right at the beginning felt harmless. They were nothing in comparison with what came next. With every new push I thought I was going to die. I urinated and threw up. It felt as if an enormous brick in my belly were pushing its way out. Slowly, very slowly. Meanwhile the sun set and night fell. I was surrounded by darkness. For the first time I didn't feel that loving affection that I had felt for my child since the beginning. What sort of ruthless monster was this, raging inside me and trying to use its superhuman strength to force its way out of me?

As it was clear to me that there was no other solution, I pressed the brick in my abdomen. It had to come out somehow, I knew that. But how on earth was it going to happen? First I stood with my legs spread wide, then I crouched down. But in every position my own body felt far too narrow and delicate for another human being to pass through it. It was simply impossible. I would burst!

I pushed and pushed. My vagina dilated as the child's head pushed against it from above. It was a terrible, terrible pain. I felt as if I was being torn in two while fully conscious.

Eventually, when I was completely exhausted, I felt something hard at the entrance to my vagina. It was the head of my child, peeping out a little way. I could feel the fluffy hair on its head. Wailing with pain I pushed on. Inch by inch the baby's head emerged. A little infinity later, with one last violent push, out came the rest of the child.

A slimy bundle lay between my legs—and started crying. I was absolutely exhausted, but also incredibly relieved. When

I was about to heave a sigh of relief, the labor pains began again and one more bloody lump emerged from me. I didn't care. My child was alive, I was alive. But when I tried to lift it up, I noticed that it was still attached to the umbilical cord.

I hesitated for a moment. I was carrying a knife with me. The knife with which Ishaku had been murdered. Should I use it, I wondered—and knew the answer straightaway. I couldn't sully this little creature with the instrument that had killed its father. I spontaneously bit through the cord with my teeth.

Then I lifted the child and looked at it in the moonlight: it was a girl, a beautiful little girl. "A gift," I thought as I rubbed off the mucus. "You are a gift from heaven. I will call you Gift!"

I tenderly kissed my daughter on the forehead. It was done, I thought blissfully: God had placed a daughter in my arms. And I would do everything to ensure that her life was better than mine.

# A bundle of hope

The birth had robbed me of my last ounce of strength. After I had cleaned the baby as best I could, I wrapped her in the scarf that I normally wore around my head. I pressed her close to my chest and leaned against a tree. Somewhere in the background hyenas were howling, but Gift made contented smacking sounds as she sucked on my milk, which smelled of vanilla. Then she gave a satisfied burp and we both went to sleep exhausted.

As soon as it was day I gathered myself together to continue on my way. My whole body was in pain, particularly my abdomen, which felt as if it was on fire. But there was nothing I could do. I had to get back to the camp. Because here, in the wilderness, Gift and I would die of thirst and hunger. We urgently needed water. My mouth was completely dry.

So off I set. As my headscarf wasn't big enough to tie Gift to my back, I carried her in my arms, which was both unusual and difficult. I must have looked completely unhinged, with my hair in disarray, still exhausted from giving birth. I hadn't even had the chance to wash.

After a while I encountered a group of five women that I knew from the camp. They had been my neighbors there. In the camp they had all had husbands, but now they only had their children with them. When they saw me with a newborn child, they immediately knew what had happened. "When did your child come into the world?" they asked. "Were you all alone?"

"Yes," I said, and told them about giving birth in the wilderness.

"And ... the child's father?" one dared to ask.

Tears welled up in my eyes.

"Yes," they said. "We know how you feel. We have experienced it ourselves."

I discovered that during that terrible night all five women had been widowed. So they wanted to go back to Nigeria. "There is no protection for us here in Cameroon," they said. "You would have to be insane to stay here."

Their words made me think. They were completely right: Boko Haram had also become a terrible threat just across the border; the fighters could come back at any time. We had to seek protection from them elsewhere.

"You're only safe from them in the large cities," the women said, "in Maiduguri or Kano."

"Is there any chance that I could come with you?" I asked them spontaneously. The decision was as good as any other: I didn't know what was going to happen next. And in Nigeria at least I had a chance of finding relatives.

"Do you think you'll survive such a difficult journey?" they asked critically. One woman gave me the cloth that she had wrapped around her shoulders so that I could wrap my baby up in it. "Here, take this," she said. "If you tie the child to your back you'll find it easier to walk."

They handed me a bottle of water. My body craved it. I thanked them and took small, respectful sips.

I was very glad that I was able to join the group. Because of my weakened condition I found it quite difficult to keep pace with them. And I felt quite ill at the thought of having to travel a considerable distance on foot. But their company kept my spirits up: at least I wouldn't be wandering around this area on my own.

As the attackers had come from the north, we headed south. Eventually, by traveling in that direction, we hoped to reach the border. And we didn't have to walk very far before we reached a larger road that ran parallel to it.

Quite naturally we assumed that we would simply be able to cross the river bed, which was now completely dry, as we had done on the journey there. So we were quite surprised when we saw the soldiers. Apparently they had now started guarding the border.

The men, who wore the uniforms of the Nigerian army, met us with extreme suspicion. "Halt! Stop!" they shouted at us from a distance.

I was worried, as I had no papers identifying me as a Nigerian. None of us did. "We are refugees. We want to go back to our homes," we called.

The men beckoned us slowly over. "Are you Muslims?" they asked suspiciously. We said we weren't. Very, very carefully they searched us and the little luggage we had with us. They clearly thought we were on the side of Boko Haram, and that we might be on a mission for the terrorist group. What an absurd thought!

"Hey, you there, what are you carrying on your back?" a soldier asked me. "Is it a bomb?"

"Take a look," I said. He did.

He could barely believe his eyes when he saw the tiny baby. "How old is this child?" he asked, startled.

"Less than a day," I replied truthfully.

"Then you shouldn't be traveling!" He lowered his gun and frowned thoughtfully. The same soldier who had just been so curt with me suddenly became friendly and soft-hearted. "You can't go wandering about the place in your condition," he said to me. "Where do you want to go?"

"To Maiduguri."

"And where is your husband?"

"He's dead," I said.

Now the other soldiers who had been listening to us looked shocked. None of them believed any longer that we were devotees of Boko Haram. "If you like, you can come and rest for a while," they suggested. They showed me a shack where their wives lived. "They will look after you until you're stronger again." I gratefully accepted their offer.

So my companions traveled on without me, and I stayed with the soldiers. Their wives looked touchingly after me and my baby. First they brought me something to eat: warm *kunnu*. Oh, that lovely smell of millet and tamarind! For a moment I forgot all the horrors I had been through.

After I had regained my strength, they washed us. As we hadn't yet had a chance to do so, our bodies and our clothes were still stained with the fluids of childbirth—and we probably smelled terrible. The women brought a barrel of water from the well behind the house. Then they scrubbed us both with a soft plastic sponge and soap.

Gift protested at first when she found herself in contact with the water. But as the women had small children themselves, they were very good at dealing with her. Soon she stopped crying, and even cooed with pleasure when she lay in the sun in the water barrel being touched and rubbed by so many women's hands. When she was quite clean, the women dried her, laid her on a cloth and rubbed her with shea butter. "That will make her strong and protect her," they said to me.

We spent several days with the women, chiefly eating and sleeping. In their care I soon recovered from the exertions of childbirth, and my strength returned. Gift developed marvellously well too. She was a very calm and even-tempered baby. It was a relief to me that she knew nothing about her father's death and the tragic circumstances of her birth. This little person seemed completely contented with me and the world, as long as she lay at my breast. Sometimes I envied her peace of mind.

Eventually I felt that I was in danger of outstaying my welcome. After all, these were not rich people. "Thank you very much," I said to them. "I will continue on my way tomorrow."

"Where will you go?" they asked me.

"I will go to Maiduguri to look for relatives of mine." I hadn't actually come up with a concrete plan. I just knew that a lot of refugees were stranded in Maiduguri, and that I would have to find someone from my family to support me. Because, without a husband, what else could I do?

"Maiduguri is much too far—and the way there is too dangerous," they warned me. "You can't go there on foot. Take the bus."

"I have no money for the bus."

They put their heads together. In the evening they consulted their husbands and found a solution. "We've clubbed together to buy you a bus ticket," they told me. I didn't know how to thank them.

The next morning the soldiers took me to a bus stop in an armored car. Several other people were already waiting there with various bits of luggage, large and small. I myself had nothing at all, apart from the baby on my back. Everything I owned was hidden under my clothes, so that no one could see it. It was the long knife that had been used to murder Ishaku. For some reason I was unwilling to part with it.

"Does the bus to Maiduguri go from here?" I asked the people, after I had said goodbye to the soldiers.

"The bus goes to Yola," they corrected me. That was in precisely the opposite direction.

"But I want to go to Maiduguri!"

"Then you'll have to go via Yola." It was the only route. The road to Maiduguri had been abandoned long ago, they explained to me, because it traveled right through the middle of dangerous Boko Haram territory.

I felt quite sad as we set off southward: my home in the north was still an area that had to be avoided. I hoped my relatives, or at least some of them, had managed to escape in time. But how was I supposed to find them?

After a few hours we reached the more southerly city of Yola; Boko Haram hadn't yet advanced that far. But there had been suicide attacks. The bus station was busy, some people were waiting there clutching photographs. They were looking for their relatives. Clearly more and more people were coming from the crisis zones. I looked around too, to see if I could spot any members of my family, my father or my uncle. But of course no one was waiting for me. It would have been too lovely.

At the station I bought a soup and looked to see how much money I still had: 500 nairas. The women had counted the sum out very precisely, just enough for another ticket. Before I could spend it on anything else, I bought the ticket to Maiduguri, which was about two hundred and fifty miles further north. In normal times we would simply have taken the A13, the main artery between north and south, which also led past the Mandara Mountains, past Gwoza and Bama. But now we had to take a big diversion via towns like Bauchi further to the west.

We drove all through the night. The next morning we reached Maiduguri. As soon as we entered the city I saw the refugees camped out on either side of the road. Above all, women, and very many children. They slept under trees or in shacks made of plastic sheets. The whole of Maiduguri seemed to be one big refugee camp. Gift was resting against my chest in her sling, and I stroked her on the forehead. And I wondered anxiously where we would stay in this over-crowded city.

When I got out of the bus I didn't really know which way to turn. I followed some women who also looked like refu-gees. In that way I reached a school building where the new arrivals could register if they had no relatives in the city who could take them in.

The whole place was in complete chaos. Women sat in a classroom, writing our names down on long lists. They told us we were going to be assigned to the various camps if we had no relatives. When I told them I was from Ngoshe, they told me to go to the camp near the airport, as that was where most of the people from my hometown were to be found. They gave me a number with which I was to report to the camp administrators.

I set off for the camp. At that time, in the spring of 2015, Maiduguri was a ghost town. Even though it was bursting at the seams, and people were living on every imaginable corner, the main crossroads and squares were curiously empty. There were few street traders, no motorbikes and hardly any cars. It seemed as if all the inhabitants and guests in town had put their business activities on hold for fear of attacks.

When I approached the camp, I could see the people sitting in the street from a long way off. The tent city was already so overcrowded that people were actually spilling out of it. Lots of children were frolicking around. I asked the way to the camp administrators. A man jotted down my number and pointed me to a big communal tent that housed about fifty women and children. Now, by day, they had pushed their bundles and mats to the side. I sat down on the floor and began nursing Gift.

Then a woman suddenly came toward me. I looked at her, and couldn't remember exactly where I knew her from.

"Patience!" she cried. "Where have you come from?"

As soon as I heard her voice, I remembered: it was Rifkatu, my old friend from Ngoshe, who I had always met at the well. Once a happy young girl, she now had careworn features. Or perhaps it just looked that way because she was so gaunt. We fell into each other's arms.

"Are you all on your own?" she asked me. "You'll see: half the village is here."

"And what about my family?"

She looked at me seriously. "You don't know?"

"No."

Rifkatu confirmed what I had feared for a long time: that my father, my uncle and two of my brothers had been killed in another devastating attack on Ngoshe. That day, she told me, almost the entire male population of the village had been slaughtered. "All the ones who weren't quick enough were beheaded," she told me. Her own husband had been one of them. She and various other women had been forced to watch, before they themselves were locked up. "They showed us deliberately, to intimidate us," she said. "You can't imagine how cruel they are."

"Oh, I can," I said. She understood what I meant. Neither of us asked the other any further details about her time with the fighters.

I also learned from Rifkatu that my sister Ladi was in Maiduguri. She was living with her husband in the city—and she probably had a flat outside the camp. Someone even had her telephone number and informed her.

Ladi hurried straight to the camp. She had her three children with her, two little girls and a boy of about ten. As I hadn't seen my sister since she got married, I didn't yet know her children. "This is your aunt Patience," my sister said, and her children smiled shyly. Then they turned away in embarrassment. And Ladi was a little wary of me too. She looked considerably older than I remembered. Her features were harder now. Still, she was glad to see me and immediately invited me to stay at her flat. "I hope my husband will agree," she said, and told me that he had left her a short time before, for a younger woman. But then the pastor had talked him into changing his mind. And now everything was fine again.

She insisted that I come with her straightaway. "Where is your luggage?" she asked.

I told her I had only Gift. "She's all I own."

"Then it's a good thing that you're coming to us," Ladi said, as if to herself. "You are my sister. It's the only way."

Ladi lived in the district called Jerusalem, the Christian part of town. It was a poor area. I noted uneasily that the whole family had only a single room.

That was where Ladi, her husband and the children all slept. She assigned me a place on a sleeping mat. I was glad to be able to rest at last.

Moussa, her husband, who worked by day as a security guard at the market, came home in the evening. He wasn't exactly delighted when Ladi told him she'd moved me into their flat. He peered at me over dinner and didn't say very much. But I had a bad feeling about the way he looked at me. "At the market we've just started searching women like you," he said at last. "Boko Haram trains you up as suicide bombers in the camps, isn't that right?"

Ladi looked at him in horror. And I was so startled that I didn't know what to say. "Nobody has trained me as a suicide bomber," I stammered.

He didn't believe me. "They turn your heads; you women are easily influenced," he said. "Only recently one of you blew herself up."

Embarrassed, I didn't reply. I myself was startled to hear that there were clearly now female attackers as well. And all the more so to learn that they came from the camps. Had that been the real purpose of our religious studies lessons? Would they have been planning to make me do that in the end?

"What's a pretty girl like you doing all on her own? You need a husband, a protector." He gave me a predatory look. I noticed that Ladi was incredibly embarrassed by his words. She and I tried simply to ignore him. But Moussa wouldn't stop making ambiguous remarks. "It used to be normal for a man to look after two or more women," he said. "There's nothing wrong with it."

When Moussa came home the following evening he had been drinking. I could smell it straightaway. Over dinner he was convivial and made jokes. Then, when it was time to go to sleep, he said, "Patience, why are you lying on the cold floor? Come and join us in the bed. There's plenty of room for three!"

I pretended I hadn't heard. But my sister was rigid with horror. I was incredibly sorry for her for having to put up with this. "Don't be like that," her husband said, and tried to pull me to him with his hands.

As he had been drinking, as I've said, his reactions were poor, and I easily managed to wriggle away. "It's much more practical for me to be here on the floor if I have to nurse the baby at night," I said, as if I thought his suggestion was the most normal thing in the world. Luckily that evening he was too tired or too drunk, or both, to insist.

The next day I said goodbye to my sister. She didn't try to make me stay. We both knew I had to go. Still, she felt guilty and pressed into my hand 200 nairas that she had secretly saved. "Where will you go?" she asked. "What will you do with the baby?"

"Don't worry, I'll think of something," I reassured her, trying to make myself sound confident. I kissed her goodbye.

"Please let me know where you go and how you both are."

Even though I'd tried to make myself sound strong and self-sufficient, I felt desperate as I found myself all on my own in the street again. I wandered aimlessly around. Now Gift and I were homeless. The girl had had a hard start in life, I thought: she wasn't even two weeks old. I had looked forward so much to having her, but her birth had coincided with a disaster. Would it destroy us? Or was there hope for us somewhere in the world?

I didn't want to go back to the refugee camp: among people who had seen so many terrible things, the past was omnipresent. My wounds would never heal there. Out of the corner of my eye I saw the beggar women who sat by the side of the street asking for alms. Should I join them? Beside them, under the trees, sat the Qur'an students, eagerly filling their slates with suras. They too already lived on alms. Once they grew up, would they also earn their living with plundering raids?

I was almost glad that God hadn't given me a boy. At least Gift would never turn into one of those monsters I had met in Kauri and Gavva. Even though I knew from Moussa that women too were carrying out suicide bombings, I still saw them chiefly as victims. I knew what they had been through in the Boko Haram camps. Wasn't it obvious that such a life would end in despair? What would have become of me if I had stayed there any longer?

Those gloomy thoughts went with me as I walked through the streets. I carried Gift on my back. How could I protect her against all those terrible things? Somehow I would have to look after this little girl, give her a home. But how in God's name was I to do it all on my own? I had never learned a trade. How could I make a living? No one had explained to me how a life without a husband worked.

If I hadn't had my daughter I might have given up. I would have lain down in the gutter and waited to die, I felt so weak and so shattered by everything I had been through. But my daughter wouldn't let me drown in self-pity. She needed very particular things from me: my breast, warmth, clean clothes, water to wash with. And it was my duty to provide her with these things, by any means possible. "Look after me!" she seemed to be shouting.

When dusk fell I discovered that I had been walking in a circle: I found myself in the Christian quarter again. Here in Jerusalem there were lots of churches. The biggest and most visible was the EYN church with its bright white building. But hidden behind the walls were lots of little churches of every imaginable denomination. In one of the side streets I discovered a Catholic priest. The young man in the clean white surplice was standing by a big iron gate, and was just about to disappear behind it. But I caught him just in time.

"Father, I don't know where my child and I are going to sleep tonight," I said to him, and curtsied the way you're supposed to.

He looked at me with helpless pity. "Are you all alone?"

"I have nobody."

"I wish I could help you," he said and looked at the ground. "There are so many of you … Oh, dear Lord." At first I thought he was going to leave me there and disappear. But then he said, "Well, come with me. I'll show you where you can spend tonight at least."

He led me to a shack slightly below the other buildings. It was not far from his church, behind a rubbish dump. It had clearly been a kind of box room or storeroom for a shop, but had been cleared because it was damp. That was apparent from the flecks of mildew on the walls. Two other women were already living there with their little children. They made room so that Gift and I could join them. "Where have you come from?" they wanted to know. "Where is your husband? What is your child called?"

Ruba and Talatu were very nice women, and I made friends with them on that first evening. They were both in a similar situation to mine: Ruba's husband was dead, Talatu's husband had disappeared. So they had to get by on their own. They earned some money by braiding women's hair. They were both very good at creating refined hairstyles in that way. I went with them and became their assistant. That way I learned the art of hair-styling. It's a very useful craft in Africa: it would seem that all women are interested in it. Even the poorer women in the refugee camps would pay a few nairas to have their hair braided.

That was how I spent the first few weeks of Gift's life; one night turned into many. I didn't make much money, but it was enough for us to survive. The most important thing was that I was eating enough for my milk not to dry up. It was the only way I could feed my baby. When we ran out of food I went to the priest and asked him if he could help us. The kind man never said no: he could always spare something from the church kitchen. I was, and remain, incredibly grateful to him for helping me keep my daughter alive. Gift meant everything to me. After I'd lost everything else in my life she was the only thing that mattered.

But then came the rainy season. With the first shower our shelter became very uncomfortable. A big puddle formed on the stone floor where we slept at night. We hastily wiped it away and tried to find the leaks in the roof. But because the whole building was so low, it also seeped in from the sides.

It was impossible to keep our shack dry. Damp climbed the walls and mildew flourished in every corner. There was a terrible smell and I sneezed all the time. We packed all our clothes and blankets in plastic bags. At night, too, we spread plastic bags on the floor. But none of it did any good: when it really rained, the whole room was under water.

After a few days Gift developed a runny nose and a worrying cough. I started to become concerned about her. "We can't stay here," I said to the others. "We will all become ill, particularly the children."

"But where else are we supposed to go?" Ruba asked desperately. The whole city was overcrowded. And we didn't yet have enough money to rent anywhere.

"Perhaps the priest has a solution," I said hopefully.

The next time he paid us a visit we deliberately didn't wipe the floor beforehand. We wanted him to see how difficult our situation was. "My God, a human being can't live in this hole," he said, shocked. That was exactly the reaction I had been hoping for.

"I don't suppose we could seek refuge in the church for a while?" I suggested.

He scratched his forehead. "The church authorities won't like it," he thought out loud. I knew what his main problem was: we were Protestants, not Catholics. And normally the churches only helped members of their own denomination. "But our Lord Jesus would definitely have taken you in ... Come with me, girls!"

We quickly grabbed our belongings, which were already packed away in plastic bags. Then we followed the priest through the rain to the church courtyard. "There's a shed there," he said and pointed to another low building beside the church. "You can use that. Will you help me to clear it?"

We didn't need to be asked twice: we eagerly carried the benches and chairs stored there into the church. We brought all the rubbish to the rubbish dump. Soon the room was empty—and it was dry! We happily unpacked our clothes from the plastic bags and spread our mats out on the floor. Our cupboard felt extremely comfortable. In our eyes it was a real villa.

And as you would hope with a villa, there was also a park: the church compound. It was surrounded by a high wall and actually looked like a park. Except on Sundays we had it all to ourselves. When it wasn't actually raining, we could sit under the neem tree and chat calmly as our children played under its branches. What luxury! The three of us could hardly believe our luck.

I am grateful for every day that we have been allowed to stay there in safety. From everything I've learned I know that it's not something you can take for granted. That's why I enjoy every second with Gift.

We women in the church compound—there are four of us now—still live in poverty. But for my daughter's sake I am always looking for possible ways to earn money and improve our situation. My daughter means everything to me. She helps me keep my spirits up, even if we go to bed hungry some evenings because we haven't earned enough. By braiding plaits I manage to save enough to buy her medicine from the chemist's shop for her cough. Because after our stay in the mildewed shed it has never left her. Somehow I feel guilty for that. I would so love to give Gift a healthy environment and a good future.

I want her to be able to go to school, learn to read and write and then have a great job, like being a doctor. I want her to grow into a strong, independent woman. A woman who doesn't need a man to look after her, but can manage on her own. That will make her much freer than I was.

I hope that is what we both experience. I barely dare to make plans for the future. When I sit under the neem tree in the church compound with my daughter in my arms, I'm only too aware that our happiness could end at any time.

Recently I parted company with the long knife that my husband was killed with. After carrying the murder weapon around with me for months, in the end I decided to leave that part of my story behind. At first I considered selling it. But who would I sell it to? At any rate I had to make sure that no one else was killed with it. That's why I finally dropped it into the public septic tank in a refugee camp.

But our safety in Maiduguri remains uncertain. The terror goes on, in a different place every day. Sometimes the suicide bombers" explosives go off in the middle of our city. I can only hope and pray that my daughter and I don't find ourselves in the wrong place at the wrong time. We've suffered enough. But of course it can happen to us anytime. It's sad to admit that.

Uncertainty will be our constant companion for a long time to come. I will never again be able to believe that the worst is over. But neither do I believe that the best is over for Gift and me. Maybe one day we'll get some good news.

# Return flight—Patience stays

I can't pretend I'm not relieved when Renate and I—under very tight security once again—set off for the airport. Another hour or two and a plane with us on board will take off and I will leave this very tense place and all the dangers that lurk here.

At the same time I have a guilty conscience. I have the freedom to leave; Patience doesn't. She looks sad when we say goodbye. She is at the mercy of this place. She and all the other women whose lives have been destroyed by Boko Haram are unable to escape their fate.

They would all love to believe that the terrorist organization will soon be defeated, as the Nigerian president repeatedly claims. People have welcomed hopeful signs in that direction. In April 2016, for example, the United States committed to its military partnership with Nigeria, and the promise to share secret service information with the government: they plan to help locate the women and girls who are still being held prisoner, including the Chibok girls.

One cause for optimism is the fact that the army has been able to regain a considerable amount of territory over the past year. As they retreated, however, Boko Haram carried out appalling massacres of the civilian population—and many refugees don't dare to go back to their villages because they are afraid that the fighters are still somewhere in the area, and might strike again at any time. Unfortunately, that does often seem to be the case.

"This terror calls for stronger and better coordinated measures from us all," the departing UN General Secretary Ban Ki Moon demanded. "All regional and international efforts must concentrate on protecting the people in northern Nigeria and the neighboring countries." South Africa and the United States have sent military support to combat Boko Haram. Demands have also been made for their crimes to be prosecuted by an international criminal court.

But the reality on the ground is still a long way from that. Only two weeks after we left, the Islamists sent more suicide units to Maiduguri. It was the Christmas attack that everyone was waiting for. This time it came a bit late, at New Year's— but with terrible brutality: two women, former kidnap victims, blew themselves up. Twenty-nine people were killed, eighty-eight injured. Patience and her daughter were only shaken.

The biggest challenge they face at the moment is the stigma with which everyone who comes back from captivity has to live: the women are seen as dirty and dishonored, since it is assumed that they were raped in the camps. Raped women are treated as the dregs of society: in the social hierarchy they rank below widows. They are despised for what they have been through. There is also the anxiety that they are converted victims, who secretly fraternize with their tormentors—and will set off a bomb at the next opportunity. A new marriage is effectively impossible, even for young women.

If a woman comes back from captivity pregnant, her family will do everything they can to abort the fetus. Babies born from a union with a Boko Haram fighter often disappear without a trace. The general view is that the "Boko Haram genes" mustn't be passed on to the next generation, because they are supposed to have diabolical qualities. For that reason Patience will have to take great care with her daughter. Too many people are likely to assume that Gift is the product of a rape in the camp.

But there is a glimmer of light for them: Renate has managed to buy a plot of land. It isn't the one in Jos that she wanted originally, but she's found another one in Gurku. She's building houses for the widows there now. At the moment there is room in Gurku for fifteen women and their children. Soon she hopes it will be more.

Her association, Widows Care (http://www.widowscare .com), in Maiduguri is also coming up with many different ways to improve the lives of the two thousand or so registered widows and help them take charge of their lives again. Renate Ellmenreich is proudly convinced, in spite of all the setbacks and difficulties, that her team will be able to give them their future back.

# Acknowledgments

I would like to thank my literary agents Christine Proske and Barbara J. Zitwer for their mentoring and advice, as well as Renate Ellmenreich and her organization, Widows Care (http://www.widowscare.com), for taking me with her to Nigeria.

*Andrea C. Hoffmann*
(http://andreachoffmann.com)